ALEXANDER THE GREAT

I

Narrative

ALEXANDER THE GREAT

I

Narrative

BY

W. W. TARN

CAMBRIDGE UNIVERSITY PRESS

CAMBRIDGE

LONDON · NEW YORK · MELBOURNE

Published by the Syndics of the Cambridge University Press
The Pitt Building, Trumpington Street, Cambridge CB2 IRP
Bentley House, 200 Euston Road, London NW1 2DB
32 East 57th Street, New York, NY 10022, USA
296 Beaconsfield Parade, Middle Park, Melbourne 3206, Australia

First published 1948
Reissued and first paperback edition 1979

Printed in Great Britain at the University Press, Cambridge

ISBN 0 521 22584 1 hard covers
ISBN 0 521 29563 7 paperback

PREFACE

Volume I of this book gives a narrative in compendious form; Volume II, which is the main part of the work, contains a number of special studies. It has been arranged that either volume can be purchased separately, as a straightforward narrative may appeal to a class of readers who do not want anything further; the work is therefore in essence almost two books. The narrative in Volume I consists in the main of my chapters XII and XIII in volume VI of the *Cambridge Ancient History*, but the text has been carefully corrected and brought up to date, and a considerable amount has been rewritten, making the present narrative rather longer; my general view of Alexander remains unchanged. I desire to express my gratitude to the Syndics of the Press both for permitting me to use these chapters and for allowing me a completely free hand over the rest of the work which they had undertaken to publish. In the circumstances, I have written a separate prefatory note to Volume II; but I may say here that some such examination of the sources as forms Part I of that volume is long overdue, and that the twenty-five studies called Appendices, some of them long essays, which form Part II of that volume, do not claim to cover all the problems raised by the Alexander story; they only deal with matters on which I thought I had something to say which needed saying; but they do include an examination of the things which are really important for our judgement of one of the greatest of mankind. No apology is needed, in my view, for stressing an individual man rather than streams of tendency or the mass mind or other 'idols of the cave'.

Preface

As for some time I have had no access to libraries, I am almost bound to have missed some modern work; even had it been otherwise, what was written in France, Germany and Italy during the war is only now becoming accessible. I trust, however, that I have not missed much of real importance, for the history of Alexander has never received much help from new material, such as inscriptions; it depends chiefly on the examination and interpretation of literary texts. My best thanks are due to the friends who have sent me references, notably Professors H. M. Last, N. H. Baynes, and A. D. Nock; Mr Nock also read Appendix 22 for me, and Mr Last and Mr Baynes most kindly copied out for me extracts from books which I could not get sent to me. I thank the Council of the Hellenic Society for permission to make the use I have made in Appendix 24 of an article of mine published in the *Journal* of the Hellenic Society for 1939, and also the Royal Geographical Society for kindly sending me a copy of the article by the late Sir A. Stein, published after his death, which is utilised in Appendix 8 ii. But my great indebtedness is to Professor F. E. Adcock, not merely for sending me some references and material, but for undertaking the labour of reading both volumes in proof with minute care and making a number of suggestions which have greatly improved the book, for which I am most grateful. In conclusion, besides my already expressed thanks to the Syndics of the Press for publishing the book, I should like to thank the printing staff for setting up the book so well from my manuscript, it being impossible for me to get it typed.

W. W. TARN

MUIRTOWN HOUSE
INVERNESS

September, 1947

CONTENTS

Abbreviations   *page* x

Chapters

  I.   The Conquest of Persia   1

  II. The Conquest of the Far East   59

  III. Personality, Policy and Aims   131

Index   149

Map   162

CONTENTS OF

VOLUME II (*SOURCES AND STUDIES*)

Part I. The so-called 'Vulgate' and its Sources

The Problem. Cleitarchus and Alexander's Expedition. The Date of Cleitarchus. Aristobulus and Cleitarchus. Cleitarchus' Book. The Poetasters. Diodorus XVII. Diodorus' Method of Work. Quintus Curtius Rufus. Curtius' Use of Diodorus. Justin, Books XI and XII. Summary.

Part II. Appendices

MILITARY. Alexander's Macedonian Troops. The Short Macedonian Cubit. Alexander's Communications. The Cardaces. The Battle of Gaugamela. The Battle of the Hydaspes.

CITIES. Alexander and the Greek Cities of Asia Minor. Alexander's Foundations.

SOME HISTORICAL ITEMS. Caranus. The Gordian Knot. The Death of Batis. The Murder of Parmenion. The Alleged Massacre of the Branchidae. Alexander and the Ganges.

Contents of Volume II

· DOCUMENTARY. The Speeches in Arrian (and some in Curtius). Plutarch's *Life* of Alexander. The Date of the Gazetteer of Alexander's Empire.

PERSONAL. Alexander's Attitude to Sex. The Queen of the Amazons. 'Barsine' and her Son Heracles. ΑΝΙΚΗΤΟΣ.

THE MAIN PROBLEMS. Alexander's Deification. The Embassies to Babylon. Alexander's Supposed Plans and the 'World-kingdom'. Brotherhood and Unity.

To all the friends, living and dead, who have
helped me over many years

ABBREVIATIONS

Berve. H. Berve, *Das Alexanderreich*, 2 vols., 1926.

C.A.H. *Cambridge Ancient History.*

Jacoby. F. Jacoby, *Die Fragmente der griechischen Historiker* (*FGrHist*). In progress.

Kornemann. E. Kornemann, *Die Alexandergeschichte des Königs Ptolemaios I von Aegypten*, 1935.

Pliny. C. Plinius Secundus, *Naturalis Historia.*

Rostovtzeff, *Soc. and Econ. Hist.* M. Rostovtzeff, *The Social and Economic History of the Hellenistic World*, 3 vols., 1941.

S.V.F. H. von Arnim, *Stoicorum Veterum Fragmenta*, 3 vols., 1903–5.

Susemihl. Fr. Susemihl, *Geschichte der griechischen Literatur in der Alexandrinerzeit*, 2 vols., 1891, 1892.

Tarn, *Hell. Civ.*² W. W. Tarn, *Hellenistic Civilisation*, 2nd ed., 1930.

Tarn, *Bactria and India.* W. W. Tarn, *The Greeks in Bactria and India*, 1938.

ALEXANDER THE GREAT

CHAPTER ONE

THE CONQUEST OF PERSIA

ALEXANDER III, son of Philip II and the Epirote princess Olympias, was born in summer 356, and was twenty when in 336 he succeeded to the throne of Macedonia. Though both his parents claimed Greek descent, he certainly had from his father, and probably from his mother, some Illyrian, i.e. Albanian, blood. When his son was thirteen, Philip invited Aristotle to Macedonia to be his tutor; and, so far as his character was influenced by others, it was influenced by Aristotle and Olympias, by a philosopher who taught that moderation alone could hold a kingdom together[1] and by a woman to whom any sort of moderation was unknown. Olympias was proud and terribly passionate, with an emotional side which made her a devotee of the orgiastic worships of Thrace; but she kept her son's love all his life, and, though he inherited from Philip the solid qualities of capacity for affairs and military talent, his nature was largely hers, though not his mind. For if his nature was passionate, his mind was practical; he was found, when a boy, entertaining some Persian envoys by questioning them about the routes across Asia. For physical pleasures, except hunting, he cared little; but he read much poetry, and shared Euripides' dislike of the professional athlete. His heroes were his

[1] Arist. *Pol.* VIII (v), 11, 1313 *a*, 19.

traditional ancestors Achilles and Heracles, and he kept under his pillow a copy of the *Iliad* which Aristotle had revised for him. During their three years together at Mieza, Aristotle taught him ethics and his own views on politics and on the geography of Asia, and perhaps some metaphysics; later he wrote for him a treatise on the art of ruling, and perhaps another on colonisation. He also gave him a general interest in philosophy, scientific investigation, and medicine. The last two bore fruit in Alexander's care for his army's health in Asia and in the great contributions he made to the knowledge of geography, hydrography, ethnology, zoology, and botany; the first is illustrated by the philosophers who accompanied him to Asia, and by the treatise on kingship written for him by Xenocrates, while his admiration for Heracles may have been quickened by the Cynic teaching which was already making of Heracles the ideal king, labouring incessantly for the good of mankind. In appearance, Alexander was fair-skinned, ruddy, and clean-shaven; Lysippus' portrait-statues rendered famous the inclination of his head to the left side and the soft, upturned eyes. For the rest, he was at his accession easy to persuade but impossible to drive; generous, ambitious, masterful, loyal to friends, and above all very young. His deeper qualities, for good or evil, remained to be called out by events.

At sixteen he had governed Macedonia in Philip's absence and defeated a Thracian rising; at eighteen he had commanded Philip's left at Chaeronea, and broken the Sacred Band of Thebes. At nineteen he was an exile. Relations between Philip and Olympias had long been strained, for Olympias was not the woman to tolerate Philip's harem; and the trouble came to a head when, in

337, Philip married Cleopatra, niece of his general Attalus, which, unlike most of Philip's 'marriages', threatened Olympias' position. Philip, it was said, doubted whether Alexander were really his son—possibly a story invented by Attalus' friends; and at the wedding feast Attalus requested the company to pray for a legitimate heir to the throne. Alexander flung his cup in his face, took his mother, and fled to Illyria. Philip banished Alexander's friends, including Harpalus prince of Elymiotis, related to the royal house, Ptolemy son of Lagos,[1] and Nearchus, a Cretan settled at Amphipolis; finally Demaratus of Corinth acted as peace-maker, persuading Philip to recall his son and Alexander to return.

Next year Philip was assassinated. It was the official belief at the Macedonian court that the assassin was in Persian pay (see p. 37); it is possible enough. Antipater's attitude absolutely acquits Alexander of complicity. Olympias may have been privy to the plot; but the only evidence against her is Antipater's subsequent enmity to her, for our tradition on the subject derives from Cassander's propaganda later. Some in Greece believed that the conspirators meant to set on the throne Alexander son of Aeropus of Lyncestis; were this true, Olympias is acquitted. Aeropus' younger sons were certainly among the conspirators, but the eldest cleared himself for the time by being the first to hail Alexander as king. The usual confusion consequent on a change of ruler threatened; but Philip's generals Antipater and Parmenion declared for Alexander, and the new king acted with determination; he secured the army, put to death all the conspirators who did

1 On the subsequent claim that Ptolemy I was related to the royal house see Tarn, *J.H.S.* LIII, 1933, p. 57.

not escape to Persia, and executed Attalus for treasonable correspondence with Athens; he had no further trouble. Olympias is said to have murdered Cleopatra and her infant on her own account.[1] It was her last public action in Macedonia while Alexander lived; though devoted to her, he was determined that she should not interfere in affairs, and in 331 she retired to Epirus.

Alexander had still to establish his position outside Macedonia; Philip had had no time to consolidate the League of Corinth, and the Greeks regarded their treaties with him as terminated by his death.[2] Athens was rejoicing over his murder, Ambracia expelled his garrison, Aetolia recalled her exiles, there was excitement in Thebes and the Peloponnese; even in Thessaly the anti-Macedonian party for a moment seized power. Northward the Balkan peoples were flaming up; Macedonia might find herself between two fires. Alexander turned first to Greece, as more necessary to him and more dangerous; in late summer 336 he hurried south, turned Tempe, which the Thessalians were holding, by cutting steps—'Alexander's ladder'—up the flank of Ossa,[3] and regained control of Thessaly without fighting. He was elected head for life of her League in Philip's place,[4] and thus secured her all-important cavalry; for Thessaly was still to a considerable extent a country of horse-breeding landowners[5] ruling a serf population, and

1 See App. 9.
2 On the death of a Macedonian king the crown became vested in the army till they had elected or confirmed a new king. There was thus no continuity, and every treaty, however expressed, ended with the death of the king who made it.
3 Polyaenus IV, 3, 23.
4 See H. D. Westlake, *Thessaly in the fourth century B.C.*, 1935, p. 219.
5 Thessaly did not really become urbanised till the third century B.C.; see Westlake op. cit. ch. II and refs.

cavalry was her natural arm. Greece was not prepared for resistance; he overawed Thebes, forgave Ambracia and Athens, and at a congress of the League states at Corinth was elected general of the League in Philip's place for the invasion of Asia, Sparta of course still abstaining: among the provisions of the new Covenant were that all League states should be free and self-governing and that their internal constitutions should not be interfered with. On his way back to Macedonia he visited Delphi, where the Pythia hailed him invincible.[1]

In spring 335 he turned against the Triballi, a people whom pressure from the advancing Celts had driven eastward across the Isker into northern Bulgaria, whence they were threatening Macedonia. Alexander took the coast road eastward from Amphipolis, turned Rhodope, went north, roughly, by Adrianople, and after a sharp fight crossed the Haemus, probably by the Kajan or Koja Balkan pass, though the Shipka is possible. He broke the Triballi in a battle, and reached the Danube somewhere between Sistovo and Silistria; but the Triballi had sent their families to an island in the river called Peuke, and, though some Byzantine warships joined him, he could not take it, while the Getae, famous for their belief in immortality, were gathering on the northern bank to aid the Triballi. Between warships and log canoes he got 5,500 men across the Danube, dispersed the Getae, and burned their town; this bold action caused the Triballi and their neighbours to surrender, and brought him an embassy from their enemies the Celts farther up the Danube, who swore alliance with him in a form still used by the Irish Gaels 1,000 years later—

1 This word, ἀνίκητος, became a sort of title. On it and Alexander's visit to Delphi, see App. 21.

'We will keep faith unless the sky fall and crush us or the earth open and swallow us or the sea rise and overwhelm us'; they added that, of the three, they only feared the sky falling.[1] Alexander now heard that Cleitus of Illyria had allied himself with Glaucias of the Taulantini (south Illyria), invaded Macedonia, and captured the border fortress, Pelion; while the Autariatae of southern Serbia were ready to fall on his flank as he went west. But his friend Longarus of the Agrianes on the upper Strymon, whose people furnished some of his best troops,[2] undertook to hold the Autariatae, and Alexander, notwithstanding the great distance to be covered, reached Pelion before Glaucias joined Cleitus. He meant to blockade it; but Glaucias closed in on his rear, and he was not strong enough to fight on two fronts. His own audacity and his men's discipline extricated the army from its dangerous position; then he turned and thoroughly defeated Cleitus. News from Greece prevented him doing more, but seemingly Illyria did not trouble him again; possibly fear of his Celtic allies counted for something.

A report had reached Greece that Alexander was dead, and the threatened defection was serious. The Theban democrats, exiled by Philip, had returned and seized power, and were attacking the Cadmea; Aetolia, Arcadia, and Elis were inclining to support them. Athens had voted help to Thebes; and though she had made no actual move, and had refused a subsidy of 300 talents offered by Darius, Demosthenes, it seems, had personally accepted the money—a

1 This oath was brilliantly reconstructed by H. d'Arbois de Jubainville, *Les premiers habitants de l'Europe*, II, p. 316. But his Irish parallel shows it was not in form an *imprecation*, as he thought.
2 As Longarus was neither a subject nor (apparently) an ally, Alexander's recruitment of Agrianians must have resembled the British recruitment of Gurkhas.

dubious act, which was freely misconstrued—and with it was providing Thebes with arms. Alexander was afraid of a possible combination of the four chief military states[1] of Greece—Thebes, Athens, Aetolia, and Sparta. But he showed, for the first but not the last time, that his speed of movement was worth an army; his campaign had already been sufficiently strenuous, yet fourteen days after the news reached him at Pelion he stood under the walls of Thebes, having collected the contingents of Phocis and Boeotia on the way. His presence checked any further developments, and the other Greeks waited on the event. He himself hoped Thebes would submit; he wanted a peaceful and contented Greece behind him and waited for overtures, but none came; Thebes meant to fight. Naturally he intended to take the city if accommodation failed; that Perdiccas began the attack without orders is immaterial. The Thebans sallied out but were defeated, and Alexander's men entered the city with the fugitives, whom the Phocians and Plataeans massacred in revenge for their former wrongs. Alexander nominally left Thebes' fate to the League, but the only delegates with him were Thebes' enemies; Phocis and Boeotia indeed voted the city's destruction, but the responsibility lies with Alexander. Thebes was razed, the temples and Pindar's house alone being left; Macedonia's partisans and other classes were released, and some Thebans escaped to Athens, but many were sold as slaves—perhaps 8,000, if the recorded price be true.[2] Orchomenus and Plataea were fully restored, and the Boeotian cities divided

---

1 Arr. I, 7, 4.
2 Diod. XVII, 14, 4, 440 talents, which at 3½ minae apiece (the usual price was 3 to 4 minae) makes 7,500. The 30,000 of Diod. XVII, 14, 1 is only a stereotyped figure, which recurs at Tyre.

up Thebes' territory. Thebes suffered what she had inflicted on Plataea and Orchomenus, and what other Greek cities had suffered at the hands of Greeks; but that does not acquit Alexander, and it is said that his own conscience troubled him later. But the blow produced its effect; every Greek state hastened to submit, and he showed general clemency; and though he demanded the leading statesmen from Athens, he withdrew the demand on the appeal of Phocion and Demades, the irreconcilable Charidemus alone being exiled; for he greatly desired a contented Athens. He retained Philip's garrisons in Corinth, Chalcis, and the Cadmea.

In autumn 335 Alexander returned to Macedonia to prepare for the invasion of Persia, and for this purpose recalled Parmenion from Asia, whither Philip had sent him in 336 with an advance force. Parmenion's successor was defeated by Memnon, who commanded Darius' mercenaries, but retained the all-important Dardanelles bridgeheads. Darius seems to have thought that Parmenion's recall and Memnon's success had removed any possibility of invasion; he made no preparations, and did not even mobilise his fleet or appoint a commander-in-chief on the coast.

The primary reason why Alexander invaded Persia was, no doubt, that he never thought of *not* doing it; it was his inheritance. Doubtless, too, adventure attracted him; and weight must also be given to the official reason. For officially, as is shown by the political manifesto which he afterwards sent to Darius from Marathus (p. 36), the invasion was that Panhellenic war of revenge which Isocrates had preached; and Alexander did set out with Panhellenic ideas: he was the champion of Hellas. It seems quite certain that he had read, and was influenced by, Isocrates' *Philippus*.[1] But Isocrates had envisaged the conquest of Asia Minor only; and certainly Alexander did not cross the Dardanelles with any definite design of conquering the whole Persian empire. There is a story that Aristotle once asked his pupils what they would all do in certain circumstances, and Alexander replied that he could not say until the circumstances arose;[2] and, so far as can be seen, he intended at first to be guided by events, and naturally found that each step forward seemed to lead inevitably to a fresh one. To discuss the morality of the invasion, and to call Alexander a glorious robber, is a mere anachronism. Of course, to the best modern thought, the invasion is quite unjustifiable; but it is equally unjustifiable to transfer our own thought to the fourth century B.C. Greeks certainly objected to barbarians—'lesser breeds without the Law'—attacking themselves, but the best thought of the time saw no reason why they should not attack barbarians whenever they liked; Plato said that all barbarians were enemies by nature, and that it was proper to wage war upon them, even to the point of enslaving or extirpating them;[3] Isocrates also called them natural enemies,[4] and warmly advocated such a war;[5] Aristotle called it essentially just,[6] and told his pupil to treat barbarians as what they were—slaves.[7] It was to be left to Alexander himself to rise to a higher level than Plato and Aristotle.

1 Benno von Hagen, *Philol.* LXVII, 1908, p. 113; U. Wilcken, *S.B. Berlin*, XXX, 1928, p. 578, n. 3 (on p. 579).
2 Ps. Call. A′ I, 16, 3 sq. A′ has some genuine information, see App. 22, pp. 363 sq.
3 *Rep.* 470 C–471 A.   4 *Panegyr.* 184, *Panath.* 163.
5 *Panegyr.* 3.   6 φύσει δίκαιον, *Pol.* I, 8, 1256 b, 25.
7 Fr. 658 Rose = Plut. *de Alex. fort.* I, 329 B; cf. *Pol.* I, 2, 1252 b, 9, III, 14, 1285 a, 20.

In the spring of 334 Alexander crossed the Dardanelles, as commander-in-chief of the army[1] of Macedonia and the League of Corinth, with something over 30,000 foot and over 5,000 horse. He left Antipater with (probably) 9,000 foot and a few horse[2] as his general in Europe, to govern Macedonia and Thrace, act as deputy Hegemon of the League of Corinth in his place, supervise the affairs of Greece, and keep Olympias quiet, a more difficult task. Of Alexander's infantry, 12,000 were Macedonians, viz. the phalanx, 9,000, in six territorial battalions, and the hypaspists, 3,000, in three battalions; and 12,000 were Greeks, composed of allies (League hoplites) and mercenaries (partly peltasts). The remaining infantry were light-armed: Agrianian javelin-men, Cretan archers, and Thracians. Generally speaking, the League infantry was used mainly for garrisons and communications; but the Cretan archers, who were not League troops, were as indispensable as the Agrianians themselves, and their loss of five commanders successively[3] shows how heavily they were engaged. The phalanx was a far more flexible body than the later phalanx, and it is now certain that their spears were not more than 13 to 14 ft. long.[4] The hypaspists[5] were as heavily armed as the phalanx, and shared the heavy infantry work. The difference between the two corps lay, not in armament, but in history and recruitment; the phalanx was the national Macedonian levy, while the hypaspists were King's troops; one of their battalions, the *agēma*, was Alexander's foot-guard. Of the cavalry, the most important body was the

---

1 For everything connected with the army see App. 1.
2 I.e. six battalions of the phalanx. He could only raise 600 horse for the Lamian war.
3 Arr. I, 8, 4; I, 22, 7; I, 28, 8; III, 5, 6 (two names); V, 14, 1.
4 App. 2, *The short Macedonian cubit.*   5 App. I, III.

Companions,[1] drawn from the smaller Macedonian land-owners who had been settled by Philip in Chalcidice and the conquered coastal district and who were the King's men; they were divided into eight territorial squadrons, and by Gaugamela were 2,000 strong. The Thessalians, also 2,000 strong by Gaugamela, ranked next;[2] there were also some Greek allied horse, who sometimes acted with the Thessalians; some squadrons of lancers from some Balkan people,[3] and small bodies of Paeonian and Thracian horse. The advance on traditional Greek warfare was to lie in the combination of arms, and more especially in the use of a mass of heavy cavalry, acting in small tactical units, as the striking force; Alexander always struck with the Companions from the right, to cover the infantry's unshielded side. But though he usually led the Companions, he led other corps if occasion required—thrice the phalanx,[4] thrice the hypaspists,[5] and once the archers.[6]

The officers were as yet largely Philip's. Parmenion was second in command; his son Philotas commanded the Companions, and another son, Nicanor, the hypaspists. Five of the phalanx-leaders were prominent later: Craterus, Perdiccas, Coenus, Amyntas, and Meleager. Cleitus 'the Black' commanded the first squadron of the Companions, called the Royal, which was Alexander's cavalry Guard; Harpalus' cousin Calas commanded the Thessalians, and Antigonus, the future king, who was related to the royal house,[7] the Greek allies. Of Alexander's personal Staff, the

---

1 App. I, IV.   2 Besides App. I, IV, pp. 156 sq., see § F, p. 74.
3 App. I, IV, p. 157; probably Thracian.
4 Arr. I, 28, 6; IV, 26, 3; V, 23, I (the heavy infantry generally).
5 Arr. I, I, 11; II, 4, 3; IV, 26, 6.   6 Arr. IV, 4, 5.
7 C. J. Edson, *Harvard Stud. in Class. Phil.* XLV, 1934, p. 213. Stories like Diod. XXI, I and Ael. *V.H.* XII, 43 are only propaganda.

so-called Bodyguards, thirteen names are known, but many were appointed later; Ptolemaeus, Arybbas, Balacrus, and probably Demetrius, were among the original members. Besides the Staff, Alexander had about him a body of men of high position to whom the name Companions properly belongs, number unknown, from whom the Companion cavalry had been developed;[1] these acted as an informal council, and formed his general reserve both for special duties and for filling all high offices, whether military or administrative, such as satrapies. They included his personal friends Hephaestion and Nearchus; the future kings, Ptolemy son of Lagos, Seleucus, and Lysimachus; and a few Greeks like Demaratus, Stasanor, and Laomedon, who could speak Persian and was to have charge of the prisoners; but Cassander remained with his father Antipater, and Harpalus, who was physically unfit for service, accompanied the army as a civilian.

Besides his Macedonian generals, Alexander had with him a number of Greek technicians, of whom too little is known.[2] He had a siege train, with engineers for constructing siege machines, the chief engineer being the Thessalian Diades,[3] 'the man who took Tyre with Alexander' and who invented (or improved) portable siege-towers and rams on wheels; there were sappers for siege works and making pontoons, water and mining engineers, and architects like Deinocrates, who laid out Alexandria; to this company belonged the historian Aristobulus, architect and geographer. There was a surveying section (the

---

1 To avoid repetition, the term 'Companions' wherever used means the Companion cavalry unless otherwise stated.
2 For what can be said, with references, see § D, pp. 39 sq.
3 § D, p. 39, n. 1.

bematists), who collected information about routes and camping grounds and recorded the distances marched; their records, which were checked by Alexander, for long formed the basis of the geography of Asia. There was a baggage train; as for commissariat, supplies were collected in each district as conquered and used for the next advance. The secretarial department was under Eumenes of Cardia, who wrote the *Journal*, the daily official record of the expedition, probably checked by Alexander. There was a corps of Royal Pages, lads training to be officers, who watched before Alexander's sleeping quarters; and several philosophers and literary men accompanied the expedition. Aristotle himself retired to Athens, but sent with Alexander in his stead his nephew Callisthenes of Olynthus, philosopher and historian; there were also Anaxarchus a Democritean, and his pupil Pyrrhon, who founded the Sceptic school; but Onesicritus, seaman, Cynic, and romance writer, hardly came out before Bactra. With them were geographers, botanists, and other scientific men, who among other things collected information and specimens for Aristotle; but many of these, with poets and artistes, came out later. More important, however, than the professed literary men was Ptolemy son of Lagos, for, to the use by later writers of his history, based on the *Journal* and other official material, we owe the best of our knowledge of Alexander's career.

Putting aside independent tribes and dynasts, and temple states, Asia Minor, as Alexander found it, was divided between two different land-systems:[1] the Greek cities of the coast and the Iranian and native baronies of the central

1 See generally M. Rostowzew (Rostovtzeff), *Gesch. d. röm. Kolonates*, pp. 240–68, and in *C.A.H.* VII, 181 sqq.; E. Kornemann, 'Bauerstand' and 'Domänen', and H. Swoboda, κώμη, in PW.

plateau. Each Greek city ruled its own 'city-land', which was often cultivated by the native pre-Persian inhabitants, living in villages; sometimes these were serfs, bought and sold with the land, as the Phrygians at Zelea;[1] sometimes hereditary occupiers paying taxes to the city, as the Pedieis at Priene;[2] sometimes their villages had even a kind of corporate organisation, as the Thracians at Cyzicus.[3] Outside the city-lands the whole soil was King's land, often granted out to great landowners, who lived each in his stronghold,[4] ruling his domain, which was cultivated by the native inhabitants of the villages, always apparently serfs. As regards the natives, therefore, the Greek system was somewhat more liberal, a matter of importance in considering the city-foundations of Alexander and his successors. But for the moment, to Alexander, the King's land with its land-tax was the important matter, for he was bankrupt. He had only 70 talents in his treasury, and his subscription towards the new temple at Delphi was only 2,100 drachmae;[5] he owed 1,300 talents, while the army's pay required 200 talents a month, with another 100 for the Graeco-Macedonian fleet of the League.[6] The story that, before starting, he gave away all the royal domains in Macedonia to his friends, retaining only his hopes, is untrue, for King's land does not vanish from Macedonian history; but he did bestow some estates, the gift to Ptolemaeus the Bodyguard being known.[7]

---

1 Michel 531, l. 28, λεὼν αὔτοικον. Cf. Ditt.³ 279.

2 *I. Priene*, 3, 14, 15, 16.   3 *J.H.S.* XXIV, 1904, p. 21.

4 Called τύρσις, Xen. *Anab.* VII, 8, 13; τετραπύργιον, Plut. *Eum.* VIII, Jos. *Ant.* XIII, 36; and more usually βᾶρις, *ibid.* XII, 230, C. B. Welles, *Royal Correspondence in the Hellenistic period*, no. 18, l. 2, no. 20, l. 5, and see p. 230.

5 See App. 21.   6 Beloch's reckoning, *Gr. Gesch.*² III, 1, p. 43.

7 Ditt.³ 332.

The Persian army was conditioned by the Persian land-system, which obtained not only in Asia Minor but in northern Syria and Armenia, and probably throughout all Iran. The Persians had abandoned their native system of warfare, which had consisted in disordering the enemy by archery fire and then charging him with cavalry; and the Persian archers had become a subordinate arm.[1] The empire had plenty of good cavalry, for each landowner maintained a cavalry troop of retainers; but infantry meant either half-armed serfs, with no interest in fighting, or hill tribesmen, brave but undisciplined. An attempt, which failed, was made at Issus to arm and put in line the young Persians doing their training, called Cardaces;[2] but the empire had really come to depend for infantry on Greek mercenaries. The course of Alexander's battles, and the large number of mercenaries still available for him to recruit, show that Darius most certainly had not the 50,000 Greeks of tradition; but Memnon probably had at least 20,000, a large force, though some were probably peltasts.

While Parmenion brought the army across the Dardanelles, Alexander, in imitation of Achilles, landed at Ilium, sacrificed in the old temple of Athena, and brought away the sacred shield which was to save his life. He declared Ilium free, restored democracy, and abolished the tribute paid to Persia; then he rejoined his army, and marched up the coast past Lampsacus, to meet the force which the coastal satraps, Arsites of Hellespontine Phrygia and Spithridates of Lydia, with Mithrobarzanes of Cappadocia and Atizyes of Phrygia, had hastily collected to oppose him. Tradition gives them 20,000 cavalry and

1 Their day ended at Plataea.   2 See App. 4.

15

20,000 Greek mercenaries; but Alexander's small losses at the Granicus show that there were certainly not 20,000 well-trained Greeks there. The greater part of Memnon's 20,000 Greeks had in fact been assigned to the fleet, while strong bodies garrisoned Miletus and Halicarnassus. The satraps and the barons with them had their own cavalry, strength unknown, a small body of Greeks still with Memnon, who had joined them, and some native infantry. Memnon proposed to retire before Alexander, waste the country, and wait for Darius; that he also advised carrying the war into Greece is unlikely, for he did not do this when later he had the power; it represents what the Greek mercenary commanders hoped. Arsites however refused to allow his satrapy to be laid waste. The Persian leaders had in fact a very gallant plan; they meant if possible to strangle the war at birth by killing Alexander. They massed their cavalry on the steep bank of the lower Granicus, put the Greeks behind them, and waited. It has often been explained since that this was not the way to hold a river-bank; but that was not their intention.

Alexander's army was in what became his regular battle-order; on the left, Parmenion with the Thessalian, Greek, and Thracian horse; then the phalanx, then the hypaspists; on the right, beyond the hypaspists, himself with the Companions, lancers, Paeonians, Agrianians, and Cretans. Parmenion advised caution; but Alexander saw the disparity of strength, and rejected the advice. The ensuing battle was fought mainly by his right wing. He ordered some cavalry across, and then charged through the river himself, conspicuous by the white wings on his helmet. The Persian leaders concentrated on him and threw away their lives freely in a desperate attempt to kill him; at one moment they almost succeeded, and Cleitus' promptitude alone saved Alexander from Spithridates' scimitar. Finally the Persians broke; their men, armed only with javelins, were unequally matched with Alexander's heavy cavalry, who (except the lancers) used short spears. The rest of the army had crossed, and Alexander surrounded the Greeks and killed all but 2,000, whom he sent in chains to forced labour in Macedonia as traitors to the League; among them were some Athenians. Eight Persian notables of high rank were killed; Memnon escaped. Alexander's losses are usually just propaganda figures, but that the Companions lost only 25 men in this battle is guaranteed by their statues erected at Dium;[1] and he emphasised the fact that he was general of the League by sending 300 Persian panoplies to Athens, with a dedication from 'Alexander and the Greeks, except the Spartans'. He left Calas as satrap of Hellespontine Phrygia, with a force of Greek allies, to secure the Dardanelles crossing; gave the vacant command of the Thessalians to Alexander the Lyncestian; and turned southward towards Ionia.

The Persians ruled the Greek towns by means of tyrants or friendly oligarchies, with occasional garrisons—precisely the method which Antipater, in Alexander's interest, was using in Greece. Alexander in Asia adopted the opposite method, the support of free democratic government.[2] Partly this was due to circumstances: Persia's foes were his friends. But it must also have been due to conviction, for he never altered his policy when he could have done so. Consequently we get here, for the first time, the opposition between the two ways of treating Greek cities, the way of

1 Arr. 1, 16, 4.
2 On Alexander's relations with the Greek cities of Asia, see App. 7.

Antipater and the way of Alexander, which was to divide the Macedonian world till 301. Alexander now gave out that he had come to overthrow the oligarchies, restore democracy, give back to each city its own laws, and abolish the tribute paid to Persia;[1] and in city after city the democrats overthrew the pro-Persian government. He himself occupied Ephesus; Priene admitted Antigonus; Alcimachus was sent to liberate the Aeolian towns; Sardis was surrendered by the governor Mithrines. Alexander made Asander satrap of Lydia, and garrisoned Sardis; but he gave to the Lydians the right to be judged by their own native laws. At Miletus, however, the garrison closed the gates and stood a siege. The Persian fleet, said to be 400 strong, at last appeared off the city; but the fleet of the League, 160 ships, anticipated it by three days and blocked the harbour. The Persians offered battle; Parmenion advised Alexander to fight, and offered to lead the fleet himself. But Alexander would not risk the moral consequences of defeat; he said he would not throw away his men's lives, but would conquer the Persian fleet on land. Miletus he took by assault; 300 mercenaries escaped to an island, and he gave them terms and took them into his service. He already saw that the purely Panhellenic policy of Granicus would not do. The Persian fleet retired to Halicarnassus, and Alexander dismissed his own, except the Athenian contingent; it served no purpose, and he had no money.

At first sight it looks as if, with the Persian fleet commanding the Aegean, Alexander was engaged in a mere gamble; Memnon, who was soon after appointed commander-in-chief of the fleet and the coast, might cut his

[1] Arr. I, 18, 2; see App. 7, I, pp. 207 sqq.

communications at the Dardanelles, or raise Greece. But in fact Alexander, in this critical decision, showed fine judgment. His communications were not seriously endangered; galleys, with limited cruising powers and helpless at night, hardly ever prevented troops crossing the sea. To raise Greece was, he judged, impossible. Memnon might raise Sparta; but Sparta was as unpopular as Macedonia, and could be dealt with by Antipater. To raise Greece meant first winning Athens, the only city which might form a large combination; and Alexander judged the situation at Athens correctly (see *C.A.H.* VI, pp. 443 sq.). Moreover, he held as hostages twenty Athenian ships and his Athenian prisoners, while in the allied troops he virtually had hostages for every state in the League. But there was more than this. In deciding to conquer the Persian fleet on land, he did not merely mean depriving it of bases; it might seize a base, as it did at Mitylene. But his proclamation of democracy had shaken the Greek half of the fleet to its foundations; for each city's squadron was manned from the poorer democrats, and would slip away home when its city was freed. And, thanks to Ochus, the Cyprians and all the Phoenicians except Tyre were disaffected (see *C.A.H.* VI, p. 22). Memnon's hands were tied; possibly the Tyrian was the only really loyal contingent he had. Alexander judged that if he secured the coast cities the fleet would die of dry rot; and it did.

He next entered Caria, where he was welcomed by Ada, Idrieus' widow and sister of the former dynast and satrap Mausolus. She had been dispossessed of her authority by her brother Pixodarus; she adopted Alexander as her son and put her fortress of Alinda into his hands. But Alexander was held up by Halicarnassus, where Memnon himself commanded the garrison; with him were Orontopates, satrap of Caria, Pixodarus' successor, and some Macedonian exiles. Alexander had to bring up his siege-train and attack Halicarnassus in form. The besieged fought well; in various sallies they burnt part of the siege-train, and killed Ptolemaeus the Bodyguard and other officers; and when the town finally became untenable, they fired their magazines and escaped, Memnon to the fleet, Orontopates to the fortress of Salmacis. Alexander restored Ada to her satrapy and left one Ptolemaeus[1] with 3,200 mercenaries to reduce Caria, where Orontopates still held several places. The Carian satrap, possibly with help from Agis of Sparta, made a good fight; he was defeated shortly before Issus by Ptolemaeus and Asander, but the reduction of Caria was not completed till 332.

Winter had now begun. Alexander sent home the newly married men of the army on furlough, a most popular measure; detached Parmenion with the heavy cavalry, the allies, and the siege and baggage trains, to await him in Phrygia; and himself with the rest of the army undertook a winter campaign in the mountains of Lycia and Pisidia. It became his usual practice to attack hill tribes in winter, when the snow confined them to the valleys and made them manageable. He first entered the Milyad, received the surrender of the Lycian towns, and was welcomed by Phaselis in Pamphylia. There he heard that Darius had offered Alexander of Lyncestis the crown of Macedonia and 1,000 gold talents to kill him; whether the report was true or not, the Lyncestian could not be left in command of the Thessalians. Craterus' brother Amphoterus made his

1 It is impossible to identify this Ptolemaeus; not the son of Lagos. Several of the name are known.

way to Parmenion through the hill tribes with a native guide, and the Lyncestian was arrested and imprisoned.

Alexander made Nearchus satrap of Lycia and Pamphylia, garrisoned Phaselis to protect it from the Persian fleet, sent part of his force to Perge by the famous Climax or Ladder—rock-steps cut in the hill which his Thracians had rendered feasible—and went with the rest by the direct way along the coast. Here the cliffs of Mount Climax came down to the sea; with a north wind it was feasible to go by the beach, but with a south wind the sea made this impossible. The wind, which had been south, shifted at the right moment, and he had a swift and easy passage, though the men had to wade; the shifting of the wind was regarded as a sign of divine favour,[1] like Cyrus' fording of the Euphrates.[2] He received the adhesion of Perge, Aspendus, and Side, and then entered the mountains of Pisidia, making for Termessus, the fortress which commanded the passes from Phaselis into the Milyad. To attack it without siege-engines was however, he saw, impossible. He fought his way north through the tribes, and took and razed Sagalassus and some forts; but he did not reduce Pisidia, though he nominally added the western half to Nearchus' satrapy; eastern Pisidia he never saw. Leaving the hills, he marched by Lake Buldur to Celaenae. Its Carian garrison agreed to surrender, if not relieved by a certain day; he left Antigonus as satrap of Phrygia with 1,500 mercenaries to watch Celaenae, which surrendered, and in spring rejoined Parmenion at Gordium. Here was shown the chariot of Gordias, founder of the old Phrygian monarchy, with the yoke lashed to the pole by cornel-

---

1 On this story see App. 22, p. 357, and the Note at the end of that Appendix.
2 Xen. *Anab.* I, 4, 18.

bark in an involved knot; local legend said that the man who untied the knot would rule Asia. The story that Alexander cut the knot with his sword is certainly untrue, but has become too famous ever to be displaced.[1] The men on furlough now rejoined, bringing 3,000 Macedonians and 650 horse as reinforcements; and ambassadors came from Athens to request the return of the prisoners. Alexander would not part with his hostages while the Persian fleet was in being; he told the Athenians to ask him again when things were more settled.

They were by no means settled as yet, for Memnon with the fleet was showing considerable activity; he had partisans in every city, and a fair force of Greek mercenaries. The oligarchs had put Chios into his hands, and he was besieging Mitylene. Some believed that he would cross to Greece; but this is improbable, for he was doubtless well-informed as to the policy of Athens. Probably his aim was to recover what cities he could and perhaps capture the bridge-head at Abydos, thus compelling Alexander to detach troops which he could not spare. Then Memnon died. Whether this meant much to Alexander cannot be said, for Memnon's capacity has to be taken on trust, and his nephew, Artabazus' son Pharnabazus, who succeeded him, knew his plans. Mitylene surrendered, on terms that she was to become Darius' ally according to the Peace of Antalcidas; Pharnabazus garrisoned the city, set up a tyrant, and levied a war contribution. He also recovered Tenedos and the rest of Lesbos, and set up a tyrant in Methymna. Alexander was forced to take measures to counter him, and sent Amphoterus and Hegelochus to the

---

[1] Fully considered in App. 10. The sword story not only makes Alexander cheat (on this see § E, p. 54), but makes him lie to heaven as well.

Dardanelles to collect ships from the allied cities and re-form the fleet. The decision however came from Darius, who was at last collecting an army; he confirmed Pharnabazus' command, but also sent Mentor's son Thymondas to bring him the mercenaries from the fleet. Thymondas shipped them to Tripolis in Phoenicia, and they joined Darius, leaving Pharnabazus crippled; he had only 1,500 men left, and his fleet began to break up.

From Gordium Alexander proceeded to Ancyra (Ankara), and there received envoys from Paphlagonia, now independent; they asked him not to invade their country, and offered formal submission. Alexander, whose aim was to meet Darius, had no intention of invading Paphlagonia; he added the country nominally to Calas' satrapy, and turned south. Ariarathes, the independent Persian dynast of northern Cappadocia, was not disturbed, and though Alexander marched through southern Cappadocia he made no attempt to conquer it; he left as 'satrap' one Sabiktas, possibly a local baron commissioned to do what he could, and pushed on towards the Cilician Gates. Properly held, the pass was impregnable. But Alexander hurried on in advance with the hypaspists, Agrianians, and archers, and reached it long before he was expected; the defenders had a panic, and he captured the Gates without the loss of a man. Through the Gates he descended into Cilicia, and hearing that the Persians meant to destroy Tarsus he galloped straight there with the cavalry and reached it in time. Here his exertions, or a bath in the Cydnus when heated, brought on a severe fever. His friend and physician, Philippus of Acarnania, was about to administer a draught when a letter arrived from Parmenion warning Alexander that Philippus had been bribed by Darius to poison him.

Alexander, whose confidence in his friends was as yet unshakeable, handed Philippus the letter to read while he drank; Philippus read it and merely remarked to Alexander that he would recover provided he followed his advice.

Alexander, after his recovery, sent Parmenion forward to occupy the passes—Kara-kapu leading from Cilicia into the little plain of Issus, and the 'pillar of Jonah' leading out of that plain towards Syria; whether he also occupied the Syrian Gates beyond Myriandrus is uncertain. Alexander himself took over the Cilician cities, and campaigned for a week in the foot-hills of Taurus to secure his flank; then, hearing that Darius was at Sochi in Syria, beyond the Syrian Gates, he left his sick and wounded at Issus, joined Parmenion, crossed the Jonah pass, and entered Myriandrus. For some reason unknown his intelligence was at fault; he believed Darius to be still at Sochi.

Darius was not at Sochi. He had waited some time, and had concluded that Alexander, of whose illness he was ignorant, meant to halt in Cilicia; against the advice of the Macedonian exile Amyntas he decided to go and look for him. He sent his war-chest and encumbrances to Damascus, crossed the Amanus by the Amanic Gates while Alexander was crossing the Jonah pass, and came down on Issus, where he butchered Alexander's sick and wounded and learnt that Alexander had gone on to Myriandrus. He had come right across Alexander's communications, whether by accident or design will never be known, and could compel him to fight with his face towards his base. The Persian command at once saw that a drawn battle was to them as good as a victory. They took up a position on the river Pinarus (probably the Deli, the distance from hills to sea being less than to-day) with their back to the Amanic Gates, their right resting on the sea and their left on the hills, and waited.

Darius' army consisted of no more than his home and household troops (i.e. his Guard and the Persian cavalry and archers), with the Greeks, Cardaces, and some light-armed. It did not number 600,000 men, and did not include 30,000 Greeks. When two Greek cities fought, each knew the other's approximate strength; but to the Macedonians a Persian army was guesswork, and both camp gossip and literary men made flattering guesses, such as seemed appropriate to the territorial extent of the Persian empire.[1] Alexander's Staff doubtless got true figures later from the surrendered satraps, but the silence of Ptolemy, i.e. of the *Journal*, shows that they never gave them out; the moral effect on the army of the belief that it had broken a vast host was too good to forgo, and all the figures we have are mere propaganda. Persian numbers and losses are throughout unknown; but the right way to regard Darius' armies is to remember that the greatest force raised by Antigonus when king of Asia west of Euphrates was 88,000 men, partly Europeans, and that in 302–301, when every state was making a supreme effort, Macedonia, Greece, Thrace, Egypt, and Asia west of India, with mercenaries, pirates, and Illyrians, had some 230,000–240,000 men under arms, of whom probably half were Europeans. Darius' army at Issus may have been somewhat larger than Alexander's, but it may equally well have been smaller, as one well-

---

1 So long as that empire was an unknown land to Greeks, we get the fantastic figures of Herodotus, Xenophon (Cunaxa), and the Alexander-historians; once they had occupied it, the figures fall like stones, beginning with Hierónymus of Cardia in Diodorus xviii–xx and continuing through Seleucid and Parthian history.

informed source asserts;[1] it was not too large to cross the Amanus in one night, and there were enough Greeks to handle one wing of the phalanx severely, but not to defeat the phalanx; as at least 10,000 Greeks got away, there must have been something over that number. The Greeks under Amyntas and Thymondas were placed in the centre, with the Cardaces on either side; their front was palisaded where the banks were easy; they had only to hold the line,[2] and Alexander's career was ended. The cavalry under Nabarzanes the chiliarch was massed on the right as a striking force. As Alexander was also expected to strike with his right, the archers were put on the left in front of the Cardaces, while on the extreme left the light-armed were thrown well forward along the foot-hills, to attack Alexander's flank and rear and prevent him charging. Darius and his Guard were behind the centre. It was a good enough plan, had the infantry been all Greek hoplites; but the Persian command had to use what it had got.

Alexander could not believe that Darius was behind him till he had sent a ship to report; then he hastened to secure the Jonah pass, camped, and next morning advanced towards the enemy (Oct. 333), deploying from column into line as the plain opened out. His army was smaller than that which had fought at Granicus. Many of the allies had been left with Calas, and 4,700 mercenaries in Caria and Phrygia; allowing for the known reinforcements, and for losses and garrisons, he may have had from 20,000 to 24,000 infantry in action; but he probably had 5,000 horse. Out of bow-shot he halted to rest the men. His line was

1 The 'mercenaries' source' in Curtius: Darius' army is small, III, 3, 28, equal to Alexander's III, 7, 9, or smaller, III, 10, 2. See § G, p. 106.
2 Arrian II, 10, 1 remarks that this shows how Alexander had already imposed his will on the enemy.

in its usual formation; but on the right the lancers were next to the hypaspists, with himself and the Companions before the lancers, a deep column of horse. The mercenaries and allies were behind the phalanx. Behind the lancers, to meet the threat of the advanced Persian left, was a flanking force, including the Agrianians; these began the battle by driving the Persian light-armed up the hill and out of action. With this danger removed, Alexander set his line in motion, and once within bow-shot he himself charged. The archers and Cardaces crumpled up before him; Darius turned his chariot at the sight and fled. But his Guard stood, and gave Alexander a battle, and meanwhile the phalanx was in trouble; in crossing the river it had lost its cohesion, and the Greeks had thrown themselves at the gap. It was a battle of the two peoples. Part of the phalanx suffered heavily, and one battalion lost its commander; but the hypaspists swung round on to the exposed left flank of the Greeks and compelled them to retire. On Alexander's left Nabarzanes had charged across the river and driven back Parmenion's cavalry, but not decisively enough to take the phalanx in flank; and on the news of Darius' flight he too retired, and the retreat became general. Alexander is said to have lost 450 killed, and was himself wounded. The Persian loss was doubtless out of proportion, as that of the vanquished usually was; but they had a fair line of retreat, and as the battle was fought late in the afternoon, darkness must have soon checked the pursuit; they only lost five notables, while part of the army escaped into southern Cappadocia and brought it over to Darius. Two thousand Greeks rejoined Darius later. The main body, 8,000 men under Amyntas, got away in good order; but they had seen enough of Darius. They marched back to Tripolis and sailed to Egypt; there Amyntas was killed trying to conquer the country, and his army subsequently took service with Sparta, to fight again at Megalopolis under a better king (pp. 52 sq.).

Balacrus the Bodyguard was now made satrap of Cilicia; Menes succeeded him on the Staff, and Polyperchon, the future regent, got the vacant battalion of the phalanx. Darius' chariot and bow were captured, and his splendidly appointed tent gave the Macedonians their first glimpse of oriental luxury. 'This, I believe, is being a king', said Alexander, as he sat down to Darius' table; and it was not entirely sarcastic. As he dined, he heard the wailing of women, and learned that it was Darius' mother, wife, and two daughters, who had been captured and were weeping for his death. He sent Leonnatus to tell them that Darius was not dead, and that they were quite safe; they would have the same rank and treatment as heretofore. He himself never set eyes on Darius' wife, nor allowed her beauty to be alluded to before him; but he showed kindness to Darius' mother Sisygambis,[1] and ultimately married one of the daughters. Later writers never tired of embroidering the theme of Alexander's treatment of these ladies; their praise of what he did throws a dry light on what he was expected to do.

Alexander's arrangements in Asia Minor may here be considered. The conquest of that country was only half finished, and Alexander did not wait to complete it. Calas perhaps subdued the Mysians, but he had not the force to

---

[1] The stories which make her relations with Alexander almost those of mother and son may quite possibly be true, for he certainly did grant her petition that he would spare the Uxii (Ptolemy in Arr. III, 17, 6), and there is no other known case of his altering his plans for anybody save at the Beas.

conquer Bithynia and Paphlagonia; whether he attempted Paphlagonia is uncertain, but later he invaded Bithynia, which was never conquered by anybody, and was killed. Pisidia was still independent; Balacrus of Cilicia tried later to conquer eastern Pisidia and met his death. Alexander at present only controlled the central plateau west of Cappadocia and the south and west coastlands, with the through route into Cilicia; this, with southern Cappadocia again in Persian hands, meant that his communications along the Royal Road ran through a dangerous bottleneck between Cappadocia and the Isaurians of the Taurus. The Persians, doubtless aided by Ariarathes, dynast of northern Cappadocia, at once attempted to cut the bottleneck,[1] and it cost Antigonus, who was in charge of Alexander's communications across Asia Minor,[2] three battles to defeat the attempt. Probably he then annexed Lycaonia; but he was not strong enough to conquer Cappadocia, and the bottleneck remained a perpetual threat till Alexander died, when Perdiccas at once used the Imperial army to conquer both Cappadocia and the Isaurians. It is interesting to note Alexander's complete faith in Antigonus.

The Persian satraps, as Alexander found them, combined all powers, military and civil, and could coin (see *C.A.H.* IV, pp. 197 sqq.); and the Persian financial system had a military basis. In the eastern provinces Alexander was to attempt to separate the three powers, civil, military, and financial, but in Asia Minor he constituted no separate civil authorities; all the satrapies embraced unconquered territory, and his satraps were primarily Macedonian generals with troops. But he made the great innovation of de-

1 Curt. IV, 1, 34 sq., from the 'mercenaries' source'; discussed, § G, pp. 110 sq. Lydia is an obvious slip for Phrygia.
2 App. 3, p. 177.

priving them of the control of finance, and setting up separate financial superintendents. Possibly the Persian military subdivisions of the satrapies, called 'chiliarchies', were maintained and utilised as smaller fiscal districts, under subordinates responsible to the financial superintendent for the satrapy. Whether the limits of his financial provinces coincided with the satrapies is unknown; at any rate there was in Asia Minor a double authority in each satrapy. The coinage Alexander kept in his own hands; the business of the financial superintendents was to collect and manage the taxes, which involved the management of the King's land; and as everything outside the city and temple territories was King's land, they obviously exercised much of the civil power. The financial basis of the Persian empire was that the peasants and serfs on the King's land—the 'King's people'—paid their taxes (in theory) to the king, in cash or in kind. Probably, however, the great landowners actually collected the taxes from their domains and paid the satraps a fixed amount, and the satraps deducted their costs of administration and remitted the balance to the king; there were thus endless opportunities for oppression and leakage. Alexander altered all this; his financial superintendents had to collect the taxes direct from the peasants and remit them to the Treasury, and also see to the assessment, which was retained unaltered on the ancient customary basis. The superintendents presently introduced the Greek system of granting cultivation leases.[1] Probably, however, the only King's land as yet directly managed by Alexander's officials was that in the coast provinces of the west and south; the great landowners of the plateau for the

1 Emphyteusis. See Ditt.3 302, and thereon Rostowzew (Rostovtzeff) op. cit. p. 267.

present remained undisturbed, Alexander merely claiming their domains and taxes as overlord. Philoxenus was appointed over the taxes for the whole of Asia Minor north of Taurus; probably he was the superior of, and co-ordinated, all the provincial superintendents.

The Greek cities had also paid taxes (tribute) to the king. The Persian rule, though apparently not severe, was naturally unpopular; and Alexander's proclamation of freedom and democracy at once brought over to his side every city where the tyrant or garrison was not strong enough to prevent it. At Zelea[1] the citizens captured the citadel and expelled the tyrant, thus earning Alexander's pardon for having, before Granicus, aided the Persians under duress;[2] Erythrae[3] came to an agreement with its garrison, and raised money to send away the mercenaries and destroy the citadel-fort; many simply opened their gates. In every city in which he or the people restored democratic government he abolished the hated tribute. Some of the island cities—Mytilene,[4] Tenedos,[5] Chios[6] are known—became members of the League of Corinth, but this was not universal; Samos was left to the Athenian cleruchs, and nothing is heard of any liberation of Rhodes, which did not join him till somewhat later.[7] But the Greek cities of the mainland did not become members of the League of Corinth,[8] neither did any other organisation

1 Arr. I, 17, 2; cf. Ditt.3 279.
2 The story (Paus. VI, 18, 2) that the historian Anaximenes, by means of a well-known child's game, got Alexander to pardon Lampsacus is obviously untrue, App. 7, I, p. 220.
3 Ditt.3 285, cf. 284.
4 The treaty of alliance, Arr. II, 1, 4; see *O.G.I.S.* 2, and App. 7, I, p. 201, n. 2.
5 The treaty of alliance, Arr. II, 2, 2.   6 Ditt.3 283. A large literature.
7 On the peculiar position of Rhodes, see App. 7, I, pp. 214 sq.
8 App. 7, II.

take its place; the Ilian and the restored Ionian League were formed, not by Alexander, but by Antigonus.[1] Each city, as its old freedom revived, became again an independent state, as it had been before the period of Persian rule, and (since the democrats for their own sake had to support Alexander) also became his free ally;[2] Miletus, for example, the one Greek city which, under compulsion, had fought against him, made him its eponymous magistrate for 334/3,[3] and the effect of its liberation can be seen in the series of treaties it at once made with other cities, possibly with a view to assist the restoration of its commercial prosperity;[4] and the cities continued to coin on any standard they pleased.

But the restoration of freedom and democracy and the recall of the exiled democrats did not always end matters. Alexander had learnt from Aristotle that a king must hold the balance even between parties,[5] and though as regards these Greek cities he was not king, he was the man who, by force of circumstances, had to make a settlement, and he had mastered a clear principle of action. All our information comes from two war years, 334 and early 333, and the dominant facts of these years were, that he wanted to get eastward quickly to meet Darius, and that in his rear the Persian fleet commanded the Aegean; and he could not go eastward and leave large seaports behind him in a state of civil war to be a prey to that fleet, especially after the lesson of Mitylene. Consequently, in the two cities where

1 App. 7, II, pp. 231 sq.
2 On this and on the unfounded modern theory that the Greek cities became part of Alexander's Asiatic Empire see the detailed examination in App. 7, I.
3 Rehm. *Milet*, I, no. 22.
4 Ibid. III, nos. 135, 136, 137. 135 and 136 are Ditt.3 273 and 286.
5 Arist. *Pol.* VIII (v), 10, 1310*b*, 40.

his friends, the restored democrats, began to slaughter their
political opponents, he at once interfered; this, common
humanity apart, was a war measure, and has no bearing on
the constitutional position of the cities, though the two
things have sometimes been confused. At Ephesus he not
only stopped the slaughter as soon as the tyrant and his son
had been killed, but punished the democrats by refusing to
abolish the tribute; he ordered however that it should be
paid, not to himself, but into the treasury of Artemis,
whose temple was being rebuilt, i.e. the punishment was to
make the Ephesians pay for their own temple. He had
been born on the night that the old temple was burnt, and
he greatly desired to have his name on the new one as
founder, but the Ephesians refused, though he offered to
bear all expenses of rebuilding; he did however enlarge the
area of the temple's right of asylum. His action at Chios,
which had been betrayed to Memnon, was similar;[1] after
the people had a second time overthrown the Persian
sympathisers, and Alexander had decreed the restoration
of the exiles and democratic government, he ordered that a
commission should revise the laws and submit the revision
to himself, and he garrisoned the city until the Chians
'should be reconciled together'; presently he ordered that
the imprisoned pro-Persians should be released on payment
of a fine, and that no one in future should be accused on
the ground of Persian sympathies. The two exceptions he
made were of tyrants and traitors. Thus he ordered that
those who had actually betrayed Chios to Memnon, and
had escaped, should be outlawed from every city of the

---

1 Ditt.[3] 283; and the fragments of a letter given by Th. Lenschau, *Leipziger
Studien*, 1890, p. 186 and G. I. Zolotas, Ἐπιγραφαὶ Χίου ἀνέκδοτοί,
Ἀθηνᾶ, 1908, p. 163, no. 3.

alliance and, if taken, should be tried by the council of the League; while all the tyrants he took were handed over for judgment to their respective cities.

One other preliminary matter Alexander hastened to settle was the boundary between city land and King's land, in places where (like Priene)[1] this was disputed; here he drew the bounds by his own fiat. It was vital to him, for till after Issus he was in financial straits, and the taxes from the King's land were his only source of revenue. But once the preliminary settlement of the disturbed affairs of the cities was over—and this was a war measure—he neither claimed nor exercised any further authority, and sent no more orders or rescripts, save the formal documents which accompanied the tyrants handed over for judgment;[2] and the cities were of course not under his satraps. Possibly after 330 the cities gave him, as was courteous, his royal title, as Delphi did in 329;[3] but this has no bearing on their position. The limits he imposed upon himself are shown by his refusal to interfere with the working of the severe city-law of Eresus[4] against the descendants of tyrants, and by the fact that Rhodes did not become a democracy, but retained her oligarchic (or rather perhaps aristocratic) government;[5] while the temporary garrison at Chios, and doubtless also the garrison which the Rhodian government accepted, was callèd, as it was, a 'defence force',[6] to avoid any objectionable implications. Chios, like the other maritime cities of the League of Corinth, had to supply ships; whether any of the cities of the mainland did even this

1 *I. Priene* 1=*O.G.I.S.* 1; see Rostovtzeff, op. cit. p. 247.
2 Arr. III, 2, 7; the διαγραφή sent to one city is mentioned *O.G.I.S.* 8, ll. 35, 60.
3 Ditt.³ 241*c*, l. 150 (p. 381).
4 *O.G.I.S.* 8.
5 App. 7, I, pp. 214 sq.
6 Ditt.³ 283, l. 18, φυλακήν.

much is unknown, but certainly, though allies, they did not supply any troops, but only money: for the tribute there was substituted a 'contribution' of smaller amount, which officially counted as voluntary. In one case at least, Priene, even the contribution was remitted;[1] if this was done because Priene allowed him to put his name as dedicator on her new temple of Athena Polias,[2] possibly he paid it himself. The contribution, being an extraordinary and temporary war-measure, was doubtless paid into the war-chest direct and not through the financial superintendents, who had nothing to do with the cities.

All the Greek cities of Asia Minor, however, did not become his allies. He took no notice of the cities on the northern coast, which he never visited, it being useless to the Persian fleet; Cyzicus was the farthest ally in this direction. So Cius remained subject to the Persian dynast Mithridates, and Heraclea to its diplomatic tyrant Dionysius; with Chalcedon and Sinope he had no relations; the story that he restored democracy at Amisus[3] is impossible, though there may have been a revolution in his name. In the south he was confronted with cities which (except Phaselis) were not of pure Greek character and speech, and coined on the Persian standard; and no clear rule appears. Phaselis and Selge became allies, but Side was garrisoned. Aspendus, which made an agreement with him and broke it, he punished like a subject town; it was fined 100 talents, placed under the satrap of Lycia, and ordered to pay tribute. At Mallus, where the democrats rose in his favour, he remitted the tribute, i.e. treated it as a Greek town; but Soli, which had aided Darius, he fined and garrisoned,

---

1 *I. Priene* 1, τῆς δὲ συντάξεως ἀφίημι κ.τ.λ.
2 Ditt.[3] 277.   3 Appian, *Mith.* 8.

though afterwards he remitted the fine and restored demo-cracy, i.e. apparently full Greek rights. The native towns of Asia Minor were of course subject to satraps or fortress-governors; even at Sardis the people had no definite constitution, though they could act as a body for the purpose of commercial arrangements with other towns.[1]

It was probably after Issus that Alexander first thought definitely of conquering the Persian empire. The alter-native was to follow Isocrates' advice and hold Asia Minor; this meant a defensive war, for Persia was bound to try to recover the sea-provinces. With Phoenicia and Egypt known to be disaffected, Alexander inevitably decided for the offensive, as his temperament dictated. He did not follow Darius; his immediate objective was Phoenicia and the ruin of the Persian fleet. He advanced to Marathus, which with Aradus was peaceably put into his hands; thence he detached Parmenion and the Thessalians to take Damascus. It was occupied without fighting and much booty secured, including Darius' baggage and war-chest; Alexander's financial troubles were now over. Parmenion also captured the families of many prominent Persians, and some Greek envoys to Darius; Alexander released the Thebans and the Athenian, but imprisoned the Spartan, as Sparta was threatening war. At Marathus he received a letter from Darius, asking him as king to king to release his family, and offering friendship and alliance. In reply Alexander sent the political manifesto already referred to (p. 8). It began by emphasising the wrong done to Macedonia and the rest of Hellas by Xerxes' invasion; it

1 Ditt.[3] 273.

was to avenge this that Alexander, as Commander-in-Chief of the League, had crossed the Dardanelles, but not till after Ochus had begun war against Macedonia by invading Thrace and aiding Perinthus. Moreover, Persia had procured Philip's assassination, and was attempting to raise Greece and destroy the League's peace, and was subsidising Sparta; while Darius, having assassinated Arses, was not even the lawful king. In conclusion, it claimed that Alexander was already king of Asia; if Darius wanted anything he must write as a subject to his lord. This claim was only put in to induce Darius to fight; but it shows what was in Alexander's mind. He did not really claim to be king of Asia till after Darius' death, or at least not till after Gaugamela; otherwise he must have treated the satraps in arms as rebels, which he did not yet do. Besides, he knew that he had not yet met the levy of the empire.

Leaving Marathus, he received the surrender of Byblus and a hearty welcome from Sidon. Envoys from Tyre met him and offered a general form of submission; as a test, he asked leave to enter the island city and sacrifice to his ancestor Heracles (Melkart). The Tyrians were really loyal; they were not yet satisfied that Alexander would ultimately be victorious, and they were satisfied that Tyre was impregnable, as after its thirteen years' siege by Nebuchadrezzar they had a right to think. They replied that they were not receiving any strangers in the city, either Persians or Macedonians, but that there was a famous shrine of Melkart at Old Tyre on the mainland which would satisfy the requirements of his piety. Alexander at once prepared for a siege; he is said to have told his men that the fall of Tyre would mean the final dissolution of the Persian fleet, a prophecy which was fulfilled before Tyre fell. The city stood on an island half a mile from the coast, and Alexander set about building a mole to it from the mainland. Progress at first was easy; it was when the deep water near the island was reached and the workers came within shot of the walls that trouble began, while winter gales and the Tyrian warships alike hindered the work. Alexander got two siege-towers out to the end of the mole, their sides protected against blazing arrows by coverings of skins; but the besieged prepared a fire-ship, fitting long yards to the masts with baskets of inflammable matter depending from the ends. They weighted down the stern to raise the bows above the mole, grounded her successfully, and set her on fire; the crew swam away, and the yards burnt through and discharged their cargoes on to the towers, which also took fire. The arrows from the Tyrian warships prevented any rescue, and the besieged, swarming out in boats, tore down the mole. Alexander began to build it again much broader, to avoid a similar mishap; but he saw that without a fleet he must fail, and went personally to Sidon to collect ships.

His success at Sidon surpassed his hopes. The news from Phoenicia had finally disintegrated the Persian fleet, and Pharnabazus was stranded in the islands. Alexander was joined at Sidon by all the Phoenician squadrons except the Tyrian, and some ships from Rhodes, Lycia, and Cilicia; soon after came the Cyprians, led by Pnytagoras of Salamis; in all he collected 220 warships, from quinqueremes to small vessels. Azemilk, the king of Tyre, brought his own squadron successfully into his city; but Alexander was far stronger now than Tyre at sea. He collected engineers to help build new machines, shipped part of the hypaspists on his fleet, took command of the Phoenician wing himself (the prerogative of the Great King), sailed to Tyre, and offered battle; but his force was too great, and the Tyrians refused to come out. He stationed Pnytagoras north of the mole to blockade the northern harbour, and the Phoenicians south of it, where his headquarters were, to blockade the southern. As soon as his new machines were ready—towers, rams, and catapults—he placed some on the mole, some on Sidonian transports or warships lashed together in pairs, and attacked the wall.

The Tyrians, however, were ready for him. They had raised towers on the walls, whose fire worried the ships, and had made near approach to the island impossible by dropping rocks into the sea. Alexander brought up merchant ships to sweep for the obstacles; the Tyrian warships attacked them and cut their anchor-cables. He covered the sweepers with warships; Tyrian divers cut the cables under water. Then he anchored the sweepers by chains; the Tyrians had no reply, and he got the rocks out. As a last resource, the Tyrians manned thirteen warships, attacked the Cyprian fleet when the crews had landed for dinner, and destroyed Pnytagoras' flagship and other vessels; but Alexander, who was watching, manned some Phoenician ships, rowed round Tyre, and cut off two of the returning squadron. The way was now open for a great combined assault. Part of the wall fell, and Alexander brought up the two transports which carried the storming party and bridges; on one was Coenus' battalion of the phalanx, on the other himself with the *agēma* of the hypaspists; their operations were covered by fire from the fleet. Both ships got their bridges placed successfully, and Alexander and Coenus captured their sections of the wall, while the Phoenicians and Cyprians forced the two harbours. Then the Tyrians broke; the Macedonians, embittered by the Tyrians having murdered their comrades taken prisoner, could not be held in; and the rest was massacre. Eight thousand fighting men are said to have been killed, and, as at Thebes, many men, women and children sold as slaves. Some were saved by the other Phoenicians, and a few found asylum in the temple of Melkart, among them some Carthaginian religious envoys, whose presence started a legend that Carthage had been preparing to help her mother-city. This horrible business of selling captives was the customary right of the victor, which Alexander exercised twice again, at Gaza, and at Cyropolis (where his men had been murdered); but it is to his credit that his expedition apparently produced hardly any effect on the world's slave-markets.[1] Tyre fell in July 332, after holding out for seven months. Its capture was possibly Alexander's greatest feat of arms; and he offered his sacrifice to Melkart after all, surely the most costly that that deity had ever received. Tyre became a Macedonian fortress, and Sidon again took the lead in Phoenicia, which dated a new era from Issus.

Before Tyre fell, Alexander received Darius' reply. Darius now offered 10,000 talents ransom for his family, and as the price of peace the hand of his daughter and the cession of everything west of the Euphrates, i.e. nearly all the country which ultimately became hellenised. The story went that Alexander put the offer before his generals, and Parmenion said that were he Alexander he would accept; Alexander replied that he too would accept were he Parmenion. The story may indicate the first rift between Alexander and the old Macedonian party, who desired only

1 G. Glotz, *Ancient Greece at work*, p. 350.

what of Asia could be governed from Europe; but it is more probably untrue. Alexander's reply to Darius was a refusal to negotiate. Darius in fact offered hardly anything he had not lost already, except Egypt; and Egypt could not be saved in any case. Once Tyre had fallen, Alexander did not wait to settle Syria; he left Parmenion to supervise the country from Damascus, and advanced towards Egypt by the immemorial route through Palestine; Egypt, once it was his, would be an impregnable bastion which he could hold from the sea. Nothing delayed his march till he reached Gaza, which under its commander Batis resisted desperately, and cost him a severe wound before he could take it.[1] The story that he visited Jerusalem and sacrificed in the Temple belongs to legend.[2]

He reached Egypt late in November 332. The Persian satrap hastened to submit, for the temper of the people was unmistakable: they saw in Alexander their avenger. He went upstream to Memphis, very wisely sacrificed to Apis, was crowned as Pharaoh, and returned to the coast. There, on the shore near the town of Rhacotis, he traced out the lines of what was to be one of the greatest cities of all time, Alexandria; it was subsequently laid out by Deinocrates, the man who proposed to carve Mount Athos into an heroic bust of Alexander. Alexander's immediate object

---

1 On the stories of the death of Batis see App. 11.
2 Jos. *Ant.* XI, 313 to end. Some still believe this story, though F. Pfister, *Eine jüdische Gründungsgeschichte Alexandreias, mit einem Anhang über Alexanders Besuch in Jerusalem*, S. B. Heidelberg 1914, was conclusive enough. See now R. Marcus, App. C to vol. VI of the Loeb Josephus, on the ramifications of the legend. Add that the belief of Theophrastus, who so often reflects Alexander's results, that the Jews were philosophic stargazers who had invented human sacrifice (Tarn, *Hell. Civ.*[2] p. 181), should alone be conclusive.

was to create a great trade emporium to replace Tyre in the Mediterranean; but, looking at the position chosen, he may already have given some thought to a sea which was not the Mediterranean. There now came to him his commanders from the Aegean, Amphoterus and Hegelochus, who had settled the last Persian resistance in the islands; Pharnabazus had escaped, but they had liberated Lesbos, Tenedos, Chios and Cos, and captured and brought with them the tyrants Pharnabazus had set up and those Chian oligarchs who had betrayed their city to Memnon. Alexander imprisoned the Chians at Elephantine; the tyrants he sent back that their respective cities might deal with them. Amphoterus was ordered to secure Crete against Agis, and to take in hand the pirates who had aided Pharnabazus; but this was never done, for the war with Sparta diverted Amphoterus' fleet to Greece.

Alexander himself with a few followers, perhaps including Callisthenes, now made his famous expedition to the oracle of Ammon (oasis of Siwah).[1] Ammon had for centuries ranked, with Delphi and Dodona, as one of the three great oracles of the Greek world. He was the god of Cyrene; Pindar had written a hymn to him, which is lost, and the Athenians had had a cult of him before 371/0 and had built him a temple before 333/2;[2] they also at some time renamed the sacred trireme Salaminia Ammonias,[3] but the occasion and meaning of this are alike obscure.[4]

1 For Alexander and Ammon see App. 22, I.
2 References in App. 22, p. 349.   3 Arist. *Constitution of Athens*, 61.
4 The scholiast on Demosthenes said that the Athenians used it to send sacrifices to Ammon, and Wilamowitz, *Aristoteles und Athen*, I, p. 338 connected the renaming with the building of the temple at Athens. The common view, which connects the renaming with Alexander's deification in 324/3, cannot be right, for this deification (see App. 22, III) had nothing to do with Ammon, and also Athens deified him unwillingly.

Alexander consulted Ammon as naturally as he had consulted Apollo of Delphi, the two visits being coupled in the tradition;[1] he was probably also influenced by the story that his ancestors Perseus and Heracles had done the same. He certainly did not go to Ammon to be recognised as a god for the Greek world or for anything else; but he did not take either of the regular routes, from Cyrene or Memphis, and this fact enabled his journey to be worked up into an adventure. He went along the coast to Paraetonium, where he received and accepted Cyrene's offer of alliance, and thence struck across the desert. The guide lost his way, and in the tradition the party made the last stage guided either by two snakes[2] or by the birds returning to the oasis, as Columbus met American birds before sighting land. The priest greeted Alexander as son of Ammon; he could do no other, for Alexander came to him as Pharaoh, and, like every Pharaoh, was already to Egyptians the son of Amon-Re. Those with Alexander heard the greeting; the king then entered the inner shrine alone with the priest. Naturally many stories of what passed became current, but he himself divulged nothing except that he was pleased; he wrote to his mother that he would tell her alone, but he did not live to do so. Later he disclosed that Ammon had told him to what gods to sacrifice, as Apollo told Xenophon, which means that, like Xenophon, he must have asked the oracle about the success of his

---

1 See App. 21, pp. 339 sq.

2 As this story is Ptolemy's, they conceivably represented the Alexandrian serpents Thermouthis and Psois; for Psois—fortune deified—became identified with Ptolemy's new god Sarapis, who thus aided Alexander. See H. R. H[all], *J.H.S.* XL, 1920, pp. 127 sqq.; Tarn, *J.H.S.* XLVIII, 1928, p. 219. There was a lively propaganda for Sarapis a little later under Ptolemy II.

expedition;[1] but his subsequent attitude towards Ammon shows that there was something which went much deeper than that. He returned to Memphis by the usual route, and for years nothing more was heard of the matter.

At Memphis he arranged the government of Egypt on enlightened lines. He retained the native officials, and instead of a satrap appointed two native governors for Upper and Lower Egypt. His financial superintendent, Cleomenes of Naucratis, was not to collect the taxes direct from the peasantry, but through the smaller native officials, as was customary; doubtless the native governors were to protect both officials and peasantry against extortion, with an appeal to Alexander. One of the governors, however, declined to act, and Cleomenes subsequently became the real power in the country; probably the other governor died, and Alexander, far away in the East at the time, told Cleomenes to carry on the government till he could make a fresh appointment.[2] A small army of occupation was left, but under three commanders; Alexander was impressed with the natural strength of Egypt and the ease with which a strong general might revolt, and the same idea occurred to his friend Ptolemy. He also appointed a commander and other officials for 'the mercenaries'. As he cannot have settled mercenaries there himself, with Gaugamela still to fight, these must represent Darius' garrison, who had sometimes received allotments of land; probably the fourth-century Pharaohs had made similar settlements. The story that Alexander sent an expedition to the Upper Nile to discover the cause of the annual flood is probably un-

1 Xen. *Anab.* III, 1, 6; see App. 22, I, p. 355.
2 See App. 16, p. 303, n. 1.

founded, for the cause was already known to Aristotle.[1] In
the spring of 331 he returned to Tyre, and settled Syria,
appointing a Macedonian satrap with a financial superintendent; he also received envoys from Athens, Chios, and
Rhodes. As the Persian fleet no longer existed, he withdrew his garrisons from the two islands, and granted
Athens the return of her prisoners; it was politic to con-
ciliate her, with Sparta threatening war. Parmenion had
been ordered to bridge the Euphrates at Thapsacus, where
Mazaeus, the ex-satrap of Syria, was holding the farther
bank with cavalry and the remaining 2,000 Greeks, as the
advance-guard of Darius' army.

The Persian command had been making a serious effort
to get together an army that might have some chance of
defeating Alexander. It was a hopeless task to improvise
in a year and a half a force fit to meet a professional army
commanded by a genius; but they made a creditable
attempt, though they could not take the most necessary step
of all, the removal of Darius from command in the field.
The best cavalry units from the levy of the empire were
called up, and were re-armed with short spears instead of
javelins. Their difficulty was infantry. Greek mercenaries
could no longer be obtained; the Cardaces had been a
failure; they had learnt that Alexander would simply ride
through archers. Their obvious course was to avoid a
pitched battle, and try to wear Alexander down with their
fine cavalry; but as the dignity of the Great King demanded
a formal encounter, and they could hardly win that with
cavalry alone, they had perforce to fall back on the only
weapon left them against the phalanx, the long-neglected

[1] See the works cited in *C.A.H.* vi, p. 596,.D, 2, *b*.

scythed chariots. Efficient drivers, drilled to act together, could not be trained quickly; still, when chariots did succeed, their success was terribly complete; doubtless some remembered how Pharnabazus with a few horse had once by the aid of two chariots broken 700 Greek hoplites.[1]

In July 331 Alexander joined Parmenion and crossed the Euphrates at Thrapsacus, Mazaeus falling back before him as he advanced. He crossed the Tigris unopposed, turned southward, and moved towards the village of Gaugamela[2] (identified with the mound Tel Gōmel on the Khajir) where, as he had learnt from prisoners, Darius was encamped. For the battle the Persians had selected the flat plain near Keramlais, between the Tigris and the Khajir, and had levelled any obstacles before their line, in order to give the chariots every chance. Their order of battle was subsequently captured.[3] Their first line, save for the Persian archers, seems to have been a cavalry line. In the centre were the 1,000 Persian cavalry of the Guard and the Indian horse from the Paropamisus; on the left of these were the Cadusians, Susians, Persians (horse and archers), and on the wing the Bactrians, with whom were brigaded the Arachosians; on the right of the centre were the Parthians (Parthava), Medes, and others, and on the wing the Syrians and Mesopotamians. Before the left wing, facing Alexander, were 1,000 mailed Saca cataphracts from the Jaxartes and brigaded with them 1,000 Bactrians; before the right wing was a similar body of horse, strength unknown, formed by the Armenians and the Cappadocians,

---

1 Xen. *Hell.* IV, 1, 18 sq.
2 On the locality see Sir Aurel Stein, *Geog. Journ.* C, 1942, p. 155, with map, and App. 5, p. 189. 3 Arr. III, 11, 3.

later so famous, under their dynast Ariarathes, Darius' ally. The two wings thus represented East and West. Darius was behind the centre, and with him the only trained infantry he had, his foot-guard of spearmen, the μηλόφοροι, and the 2,000 Greeks; there were also some other foot, and fifteen elephants from Arachosia. Judiciously posted, the elephants might have prevented Alexander charging, as untrained horses will not face them; but probably they could not be put in line, the 'ersian horses not being trained to them either. The rest of the infantry, hillmen and such, of doubtful value in a pitched battle, formed a second line behind the cavalry. In front of the cavalry line were the scythed chariots; the course of the battle shows that there were nothing like the 200 of tradition. Counting heads, Alexander was doubtless outnumbered, as he expected both his flanks to be turned; but in efficient fighting men he may have had the advantage. As the Saca brigade, whose business was to turn his right, was only 2,000 strong, the same number as the Companions, it seems that Darius' cavalry consisted of comparatively small picked forces from the several satrapies rather than the full levy; the subsequent story supports this. Bessus, satrap of Bactria and Sogdiana, of the blood royal, commanded on the left; with him was Barsaëntes, satrap of Arachosia. Mazaeus commanded on the right.

Alexander had got together for the critical battle[1] the largest army he ever commanded, 40,000 foot and 7,000 horse.[2] His original cavalry units were up to, or over, strength, and he had three new cavalry formations, two of

[1] On the battle and sources, see App. 5.
[2] This must be correct, for whatever Ptolemy may do with other figures he never exaggerates Alexander's strength.

mercenary horse under Menidas and Andromachus, and one of Odrysians;[1] but as only one new infantry unit, Balacrus' javelin-men, is mentioned, and as his known formations do not approach 40,000, a substantial part of his infantry must have been Greek mercenaries. His system of reinforcements is obscure; but, till he left Bactra, he probably got enough drafts from Macedonia to keep up the numbers of his Macedonian infantry, though not of the Companions,[2] and before he died he and his satraps had enlisted all the available Greeks, who supplied his communication troops and armies of occupation.[3] His first line at Gaugamela was shorter than usual: Parmenion on the left had the Thessalians and half the allied horse, then came the phalanx and hypaspists, on the right the Companions. Craterus' battalion was on the left of the phalanx that day, and next him Amyntas', commanded (he being absent recruiting) by his brother Simmias. As Alexander expected to be outflanked, he drew up a deep column behind each wing, who were to form front outwards if required; on the left, half the allied horse, the Thracian and Odrysian horse, and Andromachus' squadron; on the right, the lancers and Paeonians, Menidas' horse, half the Agrianians, half the archers, and some mercenaries under Coenus' brother Cleander. The army therefore formed three sides of a square, but the flanking column on Alexander's left, the defensive wing, was weaker than that on the right, where he was himself. Before the hypaspists he threw forward the rest of the Agrianians and archers and Balacrus' javelin-men, as a screen against the chariots. The rest of the mercenaries formed a second line behind the phalanx, with

1 Arr. III, 12, 4.   2 For their story, see App. I, IV.
3 The various reorganisations (see App. 1) will be noticed in their places.

orders, if the army were surrounded, to form front to the rear and complete the square. Behind were the baggage and prisoners, guarded by the Thracian foot. Time was vital to both sides; the Persians had to win, if they could, with their powerful cavalry wings before Alexander could break their line, and he had to break their line before his left gave way. Probably he always had just enough in hand; but the honours he afterwards paid to Mazaeus show what he himself thought of the battle.

Alexander gave his army a good dinner and sleep; but the Persians stood to arms all night, a needless strain on the men. Having made all his dispositions, he himself went to sleep and slept well into the morning. The day was 1 October 331. As he led his army out, he found that the Companions were opposite the scythed chariots; he therefore inclined to the right, bringing the chariots opposite the hypaspists. The battle opened on his right with the Saca brigade riding round his flank and attacking; Menidas met but could not hold them, and Alexander sent in the Paeonians and Cleander's mercenaries; Bessus in reply sent in the Bactrians, and the mailed Saca spearhead, thus reinforced, broke into the ranks of the Companions; they were expelled only after a hard fight, in which the Companions suffered, and while the Sacas were in disorder the lancers attacked them and drove them back. While this was happening, the scythed chariots made their charge. But the Agrianians and javelin-men, thrown well forward, broke the charge up, transfixing and tearing down horses and drivers; few chariots reached the line, and the hypaspists opened their ranks to let them pass through; the damage done was not great, and all were finally brought down. The Persian line was now advancing, but the left was stretching out to support Bessus; the Persian horse attacked and drove back the lancers, but were in turn checked by the Agrianians. But Alexander now had the Companions free, while the action of the Persian horse had opened a gap in their line; he at once ordered his infantry to advance, and with the Companions charged the gap, followed by the nearest battalions; the weakened Persian line broke, and, as at Issus, Darius turned and fled, but his foot-guard, few of whom survived,[1] and the Greeks, who lost a quarter of their force, held Alexander's phalanx long enough to let him escape.

On the left, meanwhile, Mazaeus had outgeneralled Parmenion, and the battle was going badly for Alexander. The Cappadocian brigade had broken through the weaker flanking column and had driven a deep wedge into the left wing; the Thessalians, attacked on every side, were in trouble and the battalions of Craterus and Simmias were fully involved in the struggle, and when Alexander's order to the phalanx to advance came neither could move; but the other four battalions went forward, and a gap opened between Simmias and Polyperchon. Into this gap the Persian cavalry of the Guard flung themselves, followed by the Parthians and some Indian horse; they rode right through the phalanx from front to rear, cutting it in half; for the moment Mazaeus must have thought he was victorious. But the Guard threw away their chance from a mistaken sense of loyalty; Darius had ordered the rescue of his family, and instead of taking the phalanx in rear they rode on through the mercenaries, made for the baggage, drove off the Thracians, and began to free the women;[2]

1 Arr. III, 16, 1.
2 There is a story that Sisygambis refused to move. It could be true.

the mercenaries in turn re-formed and drove them off. Parmenion, however, lost his nerve, and sent a message to Alexander for help. It reached him just after Darius fled; he turned the Companions and rode back. On his way he met the returning Persians and Parthians, and barred their retreat. A desperate fight followed, and the Companions again had substantial losses; finally the Persians broke through, and he rode on to the help of Parmenion. But he was no longer needed. Darius' flight had become known, the Persian line was in disorder, and Mazaeus' cavalry had lost heart; the Thessalians with fine courage had come a second time; and when Alexander joined them he had little to do but order a general pursuit. On the other wing Bessus and the Bactrians retired as a unit, undefeated, sullen, and ready for mischief; the remainder of the Greeks also got away in a body; but the rest of the army broke up. Alexander's views of what constituted a victory were those of Nelson; men might drop and horses founder, but he kept up pursuit till dark, rested till midnight, started again, and never drew rein till he reached Arbela, 35 miles from the battlefield.[1] He was determined that the enemy should never re-form as an army.

Gaugamela uncovered the nerve-centres of the empire. Alexander, having rested his army, advanced on Babylon, where Mazaeus had taken refuge. The city was not defensible, the great walls having long since been destroyed, and Mazaeus thought he had done enough for a king who ran. He came out to meet Alexander, and was received with the honour that was his due. The Babylonians welcomed Alexander; he reversed Xerxes' acts, restored all native

1 For the trouble about the distance see App. 5, p. 189.

customs, and made Mazaeus satrap, his first appointment of a Persian. He did not, however, give him the military command, but appointed a Macedonian general to the satrapy as well as a financial superintendent; and henceforth, whenever he appointed a Persian satrap, he divided the three powers, civil, military, and financial, the Persians never having military power. But in one way Mazaeus' position was unique; he was the only satrap permitted to coin, doubtless for the convenience of Babylonian trade. At Susa Alexander deposited Darius' family, and appointed another Persian satrap. He sent Mithrines, who had surrendered Sardis, as nominal satrap to Armenia (which, however, was never conquered), and Menes the Bodyguard to Phoenicia to take command of his sea-communications between Phoenicia and Europe[1] and arrange for any support Antipater might require against Sparta. The Staff vacancies occasioned by Arybbas' recent death and Menes' appointment were filled by Leonnatus and (probably) Hephaestion. Amyntas now returned, bringing large reinforcements.

In the summer of 331, before Gaugamela was fought, Agis of Sparta, who had already given Persia some help, decided on open war; he had taken into his service the 8,000 mercenaries who had escaped from Issus, and had a fine army of 22,000 men. His presence at Chaeronea might have altered the world's history; but as usual Greeks could not unite, and having allowed Athens and Thebes to fall unsupported he proceeded to throw away his men's lives by challenging Macedonia single-handed. Soon after Gaugamela Antipater met him near Megalopolis with the troops of Macedonia and the League of Corinth, and after

1 See App. 3.

a hard fight defeated and killed him; Sparta was crippled for years, and the battle removed the last threat to Alexander's rear. Antipater left Sparta's fate to the judgment of the League; Sparta appealed from the hostile League to Alexander, and he forgave all but the chief leaders; but Sparta now had to enter the League.[1] Antipater sent to Alexander what remained of the 8,000 mercenaries of Issus; but it seems that these irreconcilable veterans were not yet done with.[2]

For the invasion of Persis Alexander as usual divided the army, sending Parmenion with the Greeks, baggage, and siege-train by road, while he himself entered the hills, it being mid-winter. He reduced the Uxii, one of the pre-Aryan tribes displaced by the Iranians and living by brigandage, and so came to the formidable pass into Persis called the Persian Gates, strongly held by the satrap Ariobarzanes. His frontal attack was repulsed; he left Craterus to hold the defenders' attention, and with a mobile force and three days' food struck into the snow-hills, relying on a prisoner as guide.[3] He took tremendous risks, but came down successfully on the enemy's rear; caught between two fires, Ariobarzanes gave way. Alexander pushed on with all speed for Persepolis, and reached the great palaces on their rock terrace before Ariobarzanes had time to carry off the treasure. Between Susa, Persepolis, and Pasargadae, he secured probably 180,000 talents in coin and bullion, nearly £44,000,000,[4] besides vast booty

---

1 Alexander's request for deification in 324/3, which was confined to the League cities, was sent to Sparta; App. 22, III.
2 For their probable reappearance after Alexander's death see *C.A.H.* VI, p. 456.
3 On the topography and Alexander's route see Sir A. Stein, *Geog. Journ.* XCII, 1938, pp. 314 sqq.
4 Taking the value of the £ as before 1914. It would be far more to-day.

in kind, such as gold and silver plate and purple dye; such wealth seemed fabulous to the Greek world. At Persepolis, against Parmenion's advice, he deliberately fired Xerxes' palace, as a sign to Asia that E-sagila, the great temple at Babylon which Xerxes had destroyed, was avenged and Achaemenid rule ended. The well-known story of Alexander's feast, with Thais inciting him to the burning, is legend, invented for the dramatic effect: it had needed Xerxes and his myriads to burn Athens, but now an Athenian girl could burn Persepolis.[1] Alexander stayed at Persepolis till in spring 330 he received the news of Sparta's defeat; then, after appointing a Persian satrap of Persis, he entered Media, occupied Ecbatana, and there in the gold and silver palace sat down to take stock of an altered world.

So far he had been Alexander of Macedon, general of the League for the war against Persia. That task was ended; as an empire, Persia would fight no more; the League had no concern with the new Great King establishing his marches. He therefore sent home the Thessalians and all his Greek allies, and probably remitted the 'contributions' of the Asiatic Greek cities. As to his own position, Mazaeus' appointment shows that he had already made up his mind. Aristotle had taught him that barbarians were naturally unfitted to rule; he meant to see. Aristotle had said they must be treated as slaves; he had already learnt that here Aristotle was wrong.[2] He had seen the immemorial civilisations of Egypt and Babylon; he had seen the Persian nobles in battle; he knew that barbarians, like Greeks, must be classified according to merit, and that the best ranked

1 On this story and the various versions see § E, pp. 47 sq.
2 For the references to Aristotle, see p. 9, nn. 6, 7.

high. But one other thing which Aristotle had taught him
was sound; it was as difficult to organise peace as to make
war, but it must be done, or military empires must perish.[1]
He had conquered the Persians; he now had to live with
them, and reconcile them both to his rule and to the higher
culture which he represented. That culture too had its
rights; but he hoped to spread it, not by force, but by
means of the cities which he would found. But then the
new cities also must somehow be an integral part of the
Empire, and not mere enclaves. How he was to unite in one
polity Greek cities, Iranian feudal barons, and tribes who
practised group-marriage and head-hunting, he did not
know. But he perhaps already had some idea of the line
he would take; he was not to be a Macedonian king ruling
Persia, but king of Macedonians and Persians alike; he was
to reconcile the Greek and the barbarian,—in Eratosthenes'
phrase to mix them as in a loving-cup.[2] No one had
thought of such a thing before; no one living could as yet
understand what he meant, not even Aristotle, who was
losing touch with him now that in some ways Alexander
was beginning to pass far beyond his outlook. Here begins
Alexander's tragedy; the tragedy of an increasing loneli-
ness, of a growing impatience with those who could not
understand, of a failure which nevertheless bore greater
fruit than most men's success.

He now appointed Persian satraps for Media and Media
Paraetacene, and emphasised the new position of things by
one great change; Parmenion's cavalry had gone home, and
Parmenion, Philip's man, was left in Media with some
Thracians and mercenaries as general of communications.

1 Arist. *Pol.* IV (VII), 14, 1334*a*, 1–10.
2 See App. 25, VI.

His first task was to collect all the treasure and hand it over to Harpalus. Harpalus had done something before Issus which made him fear Alexander's anger; and had fled; Alexander, with his usual loyalty to his friends, had forgiven, recalled, and reinstated him. Philoxenus was presently transferred from his financial office to the command of the sea-communications between Asia Minor and Greece,[1] and Harpalus became head of the civil service, i.e. of all the financial superintendents everywhere, responsible only to Alexander.

Darius after Gaugamela had escaped to Ecbatana, and had been joined by Bessus and his Bactrians, Barsaëntes of Arachosia, Satibarzanes of Aria, Nabarzanes, Artabazus, and others, including the remaining Greeks; but on Alexander's approach they had left Ecbatana and retired towards Bactria. Eastern Iran had always been somewhat distinct in feeling from western, and it did not recognise Gaugamela as decisive. Alexander now heard that Darius was collecting reinforcements and decided to follow him (midsummer 330). Having decided, he acted with amazing speed. Exactly what he did cannot be ascertained; but apparently the tradition made him cover the 400 miles to Shahrud[2] in eleven days, excluding rest days, based on a belief that he could maintain the extraordinary average of 36 miles a day. He covered the 200 miles from Ecbatana to Rhagae (Rei near Teheran) by forced marches, many men falling out; there he learnt that Darius had passed the Caspian Gates, and rested his men. He then did the 52 miles to the Gates (so it is said) without a halt. There Mazaeus' son came into his camp with news: Bessus,

[1] See App. 3.
[2] Shahrud seems more probable than Damghan, but there is no certainty.

Barsaëntes, and Nabarzanes had deposed Darius and held him prisoner. Nabarzanes as chiliarch must have led the charge of the Persian Guard at Gaugamela, and all three probably felt that they personally had not been defeated. The only comment to be made on their action is that it was too late; they should have done it after Issus. Darius had twice deserted brave men who were dying for him. That Bessus was not man enough for the work he undertook is immaterial; had he succeeded, history would have justified him as a patriot.

Alexander recognised the need for yet greater haste; he took the Companions, lancers, Paeonians, and some infantry, with two days' food, and started for Bessus' camp. He was hampered by the infantry; but he had the Greeks in mind. Even so he marched 36 hours with one brief rest, but found Bessus gone; he heard, however, that the Greeks, and Artabazus, had left him. He pushed on for another 16 hours and reached a village where Bessus had halted the day before; there he learnt of a short cut, but across desert. The infantry could do no more; he decided to chance the truth of the news about the Greeks, dismounted 500 horsemen, put the freshest of the phalangites on their horses, and started across the desert. They suffered from thirst; a little water was found for Alexander, and he refused to drink; the weary troopers bade him lead where he would and they would follow. They rode 50 miles[1] that night, and at dawn, near Shahrud, they saw the dust-cloud which meant the fugitives. Bessus was in no condition to fight; Barsaëntes and Satibarzanes stabbed Darius and left him dying, and they rode for their lives. A Macedonian gave Darius a cup of water; he died before

1 Or perhaps 37; there is the usual difficulty as to which stade is meant.

Alexander came up. It was Alexander's one piece of mere good fortune; he was saved the embarrassment of dealing with his rival. He covered the body with his purple cloak, and sent it to Persepolis for burial. Darius 'great and good' is a fiction of legend. He may have possessed the domestic virtues; otherwise he was a poor type of despot, cowardly and inefficient. The wonderful loyalty of his satraps up to Gaugamela was devotion to the Persian idea, called out by the presence of the foreign invader.

CHAPTER TWO

THE CONQUEST OF THE FAR EAST

ALEXANDER was now Great King by right of conquest; in his dedication at Lindus[1] this same year he calls himself Lord of Asia,[2] while about 331 the lion-gryphon of Persia,[3] and in 329 the title of King (which he never used on his coinage minted in Macedonia), begin to appear on some of his Asiatic issues. He consequently claimed, when he so desired, to treat all still in arms against him as rebels. He did not follow Bessus; for a group of Darius' adherents had taken refuge in Tapuria, and he had first to secure his rear. He sent his baggage by road via Shahrud, and struck into the Elburz mountains with two mobile columns commanded by Craterus and himself, which united at Bandar Gäz on the Caspian and thence proceeded eastward to Zadracarta, the royal residence of Hyrcania. His operations produced their effect, and all those still in arms came in, some to Gäz and some to Zadracarta, and submitted: Autophradates satrap of Tapuria, Phrataphernes satrap of Parthia and Hyrcania, Nabarzanes, Artabazus, and delegates from the Greek mercenaries. Artabazus, once Philip's friend, was received with honour, Nabarzanes pardoned, and the two satraps

1 *The Lindian Chronicle*, c. 103, κύριος τῆς Ἀσίας.
2 'Asia' to contemporaries meant the Persian empire; for instances see Tarn, *Bactria and India*, p. 153, n. 1. Some references for the later use of the title βασιλεὺς τῆς Ἀσίας in Otto-Bengtson, *Zur Geschichte des Niederganges des Ptolemäerreiches*, 1938, p. 53, n. 2.
3 See G. F. Hill, 'Alexander the Great and the Persian Lion-Gryphon', *J.H.S.* XLIII, 1923, p. 156.

confirmed in their offices; Alexander desired to show that prompt submission to the new ruler would bring its reward. While waiting for the Greeks, he reduced the Mardi in their forest fastnesses in the hills south of the Caspian; he probably went as far as Amol, and added the country to Tapuria. Then all the Greeks, now 1,500 in number, came in, bringing the ambassadors who had been with Darius. Though Great King in Asia, Alexander desired to emphasise the fact that to Greeks he was still President of the Hellenic alliance, and he settled matters by the touchstone of the League. The Greeks who had been in Darius' service prior to the Covenant of the League, and the envoys from Sinope and Chalcedon, which were not members, went free; the other mercenaries were compelled to enter his service, and he imprisoned the envoys from the League towns, Athens and Sparta, as being traitors. Sparta was beaten, and the sea secure; he had no further need to give Athens special treatment.

Alexander had now reached a part of the world where towns were almost unknown. The true Iranian type of country knew only villages, fortresses, and 'royal residences,' a royal residence being a palace with pleasure grounds, a citadel, and an ancillary village, serving as a satrap's seat. The great non-Greek towns of the west of the Empire all belonged to older civilisations than the Persian; and if Bactra was really a town, tradition at least made it pre-Iranian. A royal residence might have a name of its own, like Zadracarta or Maracanda, or Persepolis, seemingly a corruption of Portipora; but it was often called by the name of the province, as 'the Arachosians', 'the Persians'. If Alexander wanted cities in eastern Iran he must build them.

From Astrabad Alexander started to follow Bessus, who had gone to Bactria, while Satibarzanes and Barsaëntes had returned to their satrapies to collect troops preparatory to joining him. Alexander went up the Gurgan river and by Bujnurd into the valley of the Kashaf-Rud. At Meshed he received and accepted the submission of Satibarzanes, who was not yet prepared for resistance, and confirmed him in his satrapy, sending Anaxippus to him as general but with an inadequate force. Doubtless he was trying a policy of trust; at the same time he had evidently no idea of the feeling in Aria. He also heard that Bessus, supported by the Bactrians, had assumed the upright tiara and called himself Great King. From Meshed he followed the regular road towards Balkh; he may have reached the Murghab river when he heard that Satibarzanes had risen and killed Anaxippus and his force, and was collecting troops; Arachosia was also in arms. He could not invade Bactria with Aria up behind him; he had to turn. Leaving Craterus to follow with the army, he hurried south with a small force, and in two days reached the royal residence, Artacoana; Satibarzanes was surprised, and barely escaped to Bessus. Alexander marched through Aria, and, as he thought, subdued it; near Artacoana he founded Alexandria of the Arians (Herat). He appointed another Persian, Arsames, as satrap; he did not yet understand that eastern Iran was fighting a national war. Then he entered Drangiana, which was part of Barsaëntes' satrapy. Barsaëntes fled to the Indians in eastern Arachosia, and was handed over to Alexander, who put him to death; as Nabarzanes and Satibarzanes had been pardoned, it is clear that he was executed for rebellion and not for Darius' murder.

Alexander halted at the royal residence, Phrada,[1] possibly near Nad Ali, site of the later capital, Faranj, which preserved the alternative name 'the Zarangians'; and here occurred the execution of Parmenion's son Philotas. In estimating what happened, Alexander's position among his generals must be borne in mind. Olympias once rebuked him for making these men the equals of kings;[2] and indeed they were little less. Some were princes of old lines; most were as proud and ambitious as himself, and intoxicated with victory and its material fruits. Many of them had high military ability; a few were to be great administrators. Of things like the sanctity of life they thought little; they lived hard and took their chances in a world full of wonderful chances. And not one of them could understand Alexander. The ancient world had never seen such a group of men; and Alexander, who was twenty-two when he crossed the Dardanelles, had to drive them as a team. He did drive them with success till he died; but his success was not as yet a foregone conclusion.

There seems to have been a conservative element among the generals, men who did not care for Alexander's position as Great King, or his Persian policy and satraps. Their ideal was a national king like Philip, first among his peers; they disliked the notion of a king without a peer. Philotas, an overbearing man, may have represented this element; but more probably the motive of his treason was personal, not political. For Parmenion's family had held too much power; but now his son Nicanor was dead, and Parmenion himself had fallen out of favour. Since crossing the

1 On its position, Tarn, *Bactria and India*, p. 14, n. 4 (very full). It is certainly not Farah, the usual location.
2 Olympias' letter, Plut. *Alex.* xxxix, must be genuine, see App. 16, p. 302.

Dardanelles Alexander had uniformly disregarded his advice and had uniformly been successful; Parmenion too had failed at Gaugamela, and his enemies, including Callisthenes, were hinting that he had not particularly desired Alexander's victory. Since then Alexander had left him on communications, and Craterus was fast taking his place as second in command. Is the explanation of Philotas' action to be found in a belief that the star of his house was setting and his own position insecure?

Philotas' loyalty had already once been called in question; but Alexander had simply passed the matter by, as he had done with Harpalus. But at Phrada a plot was discovered against Alexander's life. The ringleader was an obscure person, but he claimed the support of Amyntas the phalanx-leader and Demetrius the Bodyguard. The plot came to Philotas' ears; on his own admission, he knew of it for two days and did not tell Alexander. Then Alexander heard. If Philotas, general of the Companions, were a traitor, it was necessary to strike hard and quickly. It was Macedonian custom that in a trial for treason, where the king was virtually a party, the State was represented, as it was when the throne was vacant, by the Macedonian people under arms, the army;[1] and Philotas was properly put on trial before the army. Nothing further is known beyond Ptolemy's statement that the proofs of his treason were perfectly clear; the army condemned him to death, and carried out its sentence according to Macedonian custom. It was rough and ready justice; but the army gave a fair trial according to its lights. For, after Philotas, Amyntas and his brothers were tried; all were acquitted and continued in their commands. Demetrius was sub-

1 See App. 24, p. 379, nn. 1, 2; cf. § G, p. 106.

sequently cashiered, and Ptolemy son of Lagos replaced him on the Staff. It is said that Alexander the Lyncestian was now put to death; it has been thought that the conspirators meant to make him king.

There remained Parmenion. There was no evidence against him, but he could not be left in charge of Alexander's communications. But neither could he be removed. That a great general could be relieved of his command and retire quietly into private life would probably have seemed impossible to every Macedonian. There were only two known alternatives: he must rebel or die. Alexander decided that Parmenion must die. He sent Polydamas with swift dromedaries across the desert, bearing letters to Parmenion's generals in Media, the Macedonians Cleander, Parmenion's principal lieutenant, and Menidas, and the Thracian Sitalces. Polydamas travelled faster than rumour; the generals carried out Alexander's orders and killed Parmenion. Philotas' execution had been perfectly judicial; Parmenion's was plain murder,[1] and leaves a deep stain on Alexander's reputation. But he had shown his generals that he was master; he struck once, with terrible effect, and the lesson went home; six years (p. 109) passed before he had to strike again.

It was clear that no subject must again hold Philotas' power; and the Companions were reorganised as two hipparchies, each of four squadrons, under Hephaestion and Cleitus as hipparchs, the Royal squadron being included in Cleitus' command.[2] Alexander founded an Alexandria at Phrada whose nickname later was Proph-

1 App. 12.   2 App. 1, IV, p. 161.

thasia,[1] 'Anticipation',—a curious allusion to the conspiracy. He apparently never took winter quarters at all in the winter of 330–329 B.C.; he was anxious to reach Bactria, and he had to ensure Bessus' isolation from the south. He went on from Phrada to the Helmund, where he found a people (perhaps the almost extinct Reis tribes) called the Benefactors, because they had once aided Cyrus with supplies. They are represented as an innocent folk enjoying a golden age of righteousness, and he exempted them from satrapal rule and tribute for helping his predecessor Cyrus. The satraps of Carmania and Gedrosia now sent their submission; but Arachosia was masterless and unconquered. Alexander separated Drangiana from it and added it to Aria; then he followed up the Helmund and the Argandab into Arachosia, left Menon to reduce the country, pushed on up the Tarnak, and founded another Alexandria (Ghazni).[2] Thence he crossed the mountains into the Paropamisadae[3] (spring 329). The troops suffered from cold and snow blindness, and were glad to shelter at night in the beehive huts which the natives built with a hole in the roof to let out the smoke; but the natives had plenty of animals, and tradition may have exaggerated the sufferings of the march, though Alexander possibly crossed too early in the year. In the Paropamisadae he founded another city, Alexandria of the Caucasus; it seemingly stood in Opiane, below the junction of the Ghorband

---

1 App. 8, I, p. 236, and III. For the system of nicknames (popular names) of eastern Greek cities, see Tarn, *Bactria and India*, pp. 13–16.
2 Ghazni, not Candahar: Tarn, op. cit. pp. 470 sq., and see App. 8, I, pp. 234, 249.
3 If this satrapy had a name of its own, it is lost. It is often referred to as 'the Cabul valley', which is misleading. For a description of it, see Tarn, op. cit. pp. 95 sqq.

and Panjshir rivers, on the right bank of their united stream.[1] He appointed a Persian satrap of the country and prepared to cross the Paropamisus or 'Caucasus' (Hindu Kush) into Bactria.

Bessus was holding Aornos (Tashkurgan) with 7,000 Bactrians and a force of Dahae from the desert; with him were the two greatest barons of Sogdiana, Oxyartes and Spitamenes. The regular route from the Paropamisadae into Bactria ran up the Ghorband past Bamyan,[2] turning rather than crossing the Hindu Kush; Alexander, however, went north up the Panjshir and crossed the range itself by the Khawak pass, 11,600 feet high but lower though far longer than the central group of passes; his aim was to turn Bessus from the north. The army suffered from lack of food and firing, and lived on raw mule and silphium; but they got across with little loss. The pass led to Anderab, and Bessus had wasted the surrounding country up to the mountains; but Alexander, who had no intention of fighting his way through the defile at Tashkurgan, as Bessus hoped, did not take the direct route from Anderab to Tashkurgan, but bore north again, reached Drapsaka, and turned Bessus' position. Bessus fled across the Oxus; the Bactrians submitted, and Alexander occupied Tashkurgan and Zariaspa-Bactra without resistance, and made the veteran Artabazus satrap of Bactria. At last too Aria was settled. Satibarzanes, with Arsames' privity, had returned and raised the country again while Alexander was in Arachosia, but had been defeated and killed by a force sent under Erigyius. Alexander now sent as satrap Stasanor,

1 App. 8, 1, p. 236. Excavations are now in progress.
2 Tarn, op. cit. pp. 139 sq. See now A. Foucher and Mme. E. Bazin-Foucher, *La vieille route de l'Inde de Bactres à Taxila* (2 vols.), 1942.

of the royal house of Soli in Cyprus, with orders to remove Arsames. The national war had forced upon Alexander a change in his Persian policy; but in Stasanor he had found the right man, and Aria had peace.

From Bactra Alexander marched to the Oxus opposite Kilif, the army suffering from thirst in the summer heat; Bessus' had destroyed all the boats, but the troops crossed native fashion, lying flat on skins stuffed with rushes and paddling. (The famous story, which occurs here, of Alexander's massacre of a harmless community of exiles from Branchidae for their ancestors' supposed treachery towards Apollo, is a clumsy fabrication.)[1] Word now came from Spitamenes that Bessus was his prisoner and that he was ready to surrender him. Ptolemy was sent to take the surrender; but after a forced march he learnt that Spitamenes had changed his mind and gone, leaving Bessus behind. He captured Bessus, who was put in the pillory and shown to the army, publicly flogged, and sent to Bactra to await judgment. Alexander then occupied Maracanda (Samarcand), the summer royal residence of Sogdiana, and pushed on by the usual route northward past the fortress of Cyropolis to the great southward loop of the Jaxartes, where Persian rule had ended; on the way he was wounded in the tibia and lost part of the bone. He left garrisons of mercenaries in Cyropolis and in the seven fortresses between Cyropolis and the Jaxartes which the Persians had built for protection against the nomads; and from there, at the end of the known world, he summoned all the Sogdian barons to a durbar in Bactra. He thought Sogdiana had submitted; but it was merely waiting for a lead, and the invitation to the durbar, which could mean

1 See App. 13.

nothing good, kindled the torch. The whole country flamed up behind him; his garrisons in Cyropolis and the seven fortresses were killed, and he had to reduce these places one after the other; at Cyropolis, which he razed, he was again wounded. He showed considerable severity; cut off from information, he thought he was dealing with a local revolt which severity might suppress.

At last he got news: Spitamenes had risen in revolt and was besieging the citadel of Maracanda. Alexander could not spare many men to relieve the place, for a host of Saca nomads was gathering on the Jaxartes; he sent 2,300 mercenaries and 60 Companions, under the command of his interpreter Pharnuches, a Lycian; probably he scarcely realised that things were serious, and thought there might be negotiations. Meanwhile he decided to found a city on the Jaxartes as a defence against the nomads. In 20 days the mud walls were finished and the city settled; it was called 'Alexandria the Farthest,' to-day Chodjend. All the time that the city was building the nomads patrolled the farther bank, challenging him to cross. They were beyond his marches; but he wished to prevent them helping Spitamenes, and he did not mean to be mocked by 'Scythians' as Darius I had been. He mounted his catapults on some of his boats, and thus got them within range of the enemy; the nomads were alarmed by the power of the strange weapons, and retired out of shot. The army then crossed as it had crossed the Oxus, Alexander with the archers leading; once landed, he kept a clear space for the army to land behind him. Part of his heavy cavalry then attacked; the nomads tried desert tactics, riding round them and shooting; Alexander mixed the Agrianians and archers with the cavalry, and these succeeded in stopping the encircling tactics of the enemy.[1] Once this was done, Alexander made his usual charge, and the nomads broke. He pursued them a long way, though very ill from drinking foul water; finally he had to be carried back to camp. The battle is notable, for it shows Alexander, who had never seen desert or 'Parthian' tactics before, meeting them with complete confidence and certainty; had he been an inferior general, he might conceivably have suffered the fate of Crassus at Carrhae.

What might have happened to Alexander did happen to the troops sent to relieve Maracanda. Spitamenes, besides his own Sogdian horse, had found allies in the nomads of the Kirghiz steppe west of the Polytimetus river, part of the great Saca confederacy known as the Massagetae; he retired down the river and drew the relieving force after him to the edge of the desert. There he attacked, using desert tactics. Pharnuches was not a soldier, and none of the commanders would take the responsibility. The men formed square and fought their way back to the river, but at the sight of safety discipline gave way; there was a rush to cross, and Spitamenes practically annihilated the force. When Alexander heard, he realised at last that he was face to face with a national war and a national leader. He had apparently quitted Chodjend, and, assuming that the short (bematists') stade be meant, was some 135 miles from Maracanda. He took the Companions, Agrianians, archers, and some picked phalangites, and according to tradition reached Maracanda in a little over three days and three nights; if allowance be made for better climatic conditions

---

1 It is impossible to understand, from Arrian's too brief account, what Alexander really did in this battle. Conceivably Arrian himself could not understand his source.

than to-day, for it being late autumn, and for Alexander's terrific driving power, it can hardly be pronounced impossible offhand, if the cavalry carried the spears and shields. Spitamenes was again besieging Maracanda; again he retreated to the desert. Alexander went as far as the battlefield and buried the dead, but he did not follow Spitamenes; he turned and retraced his steps up the Polytimetus, wasting its rich valley from end to end to prevent the enemy again attacking Maracanda. Thence he returned to Bactra, where he wintered; the victorious Spitamenes, with his headquarters in the winter royal residence of Sogdiana, Bokhara, was left undisturbed till spring. Alexander held little north of the Oxus but Chodjend and Maracanda; but the army had had no rest for two strenuous years, and winter quarters were an absolute necessity.

There was a great gathering at Bactra that winter (329–328). Phrataphernes and Stasanor came bringing in Arsames and other partisans of Bessus; large reinforcements arrived from Europe; the western satraps brought fresh drafts of mercenaries; many Greeks of various professions apparently came out. Bessus was brought out and judged; his ears and nose were cut off and he was sent to Ecbatana for execution. He was condemned, not for the murder of Darius, but for having assumed the tiara; Alexander, in mutilating him, treated him as Darius I had treated Fravartish. It is the only occasion on which Alexander is recorded on any reputable authority to have used torture; but doubtless his Asiatic subjects expected it, and after all contemporary Greeks often employed far worse measures than mutilation.[1] There also came Pharasmanes, ruler of the Chorasmii,[2] now settled in Kwarizm south of the Aral

1 *C.A.H.* IV, p. 179.   2 On the Chorasmii see Tarn, op. cit. App. 11.

Sea; he offered Alexander his alliance and was also understood to have offered to guide him by some northern route
to the Black Sea, thus linking up Bactria with Thrace,
which shows that Pharasmanes knew, or knew of, the
trade route[1] which ran through the land of the Aorsi north
of the Hyrcanian Sea (our Caspian) to the Black Sea.
Alexander had learnt from Aristotle that there was a second
inland sea, the Aral (Aristotle's Caspian) long before he
met Pharasmanes,[2] who knew the Aral well; but some took
that king's offer of guidance to mean that the Black Sea
was quite close, one of the causes which ultimately led
Cleitarchus and others to identify the Aral with the
Maeotis (Sea of Azov),[3] with all its unhappy consequences
to geographical study. Possibly the subsequent expedition
made by Zopyrion, Antipater's general in Thrace, who
crossed the Danube, perhaps reached Olbia, and was killed
by the Scythians, was an attempt to link Thrace with
Bactria. Had Alexander lived, he might have attended to
the Black Sea and its problems; but for the present, while
accepting Pharasmanes' alliance, he told him that he must
next go to India.

Sogdiana, however, had first to be reduced. In spring
328 Alexander left Bactra and again crossed the Oxus; by
the river he found a spring of petroleum[4] (he was the first

1 Strab. XI, 5, 8 (506).
2 See § B, where Greek knowledge of the Aralo-Caspian water-system
  is fully treated according to its proper historical development.
3 § B, pp. 14 to end.
4 Arr. IV, 15, 7, ἔλαιον. Greeks had as yet no word for petroleum, and it is
  never mentioned till much later, with one exception: Herodotus (VI, 119)
  had heard of a well near Susa from which three substances were drawn,
  bitumen, salts, and ἔλαιον, black with a bad smell. See generally R. J.
  Forbes, *Bitumen and Petroleum in Antiquity*, Leiden, 1936, pp. 29 sq. (his
  references to Aristotle are, however, to Ps.-Arist. *de miris auscult.*, which is
  late).

European known to have set eyes upon it), and offered sacrifice to avert the evil consequences of the prodigy. The army he divided into five columns, which swept the plain country and reunited at Maracanda. Spitamenes could not face them; he quitted Sogdiana and went to the Massagetae. Alexander ordered Hephaestion to build fortified posts at various points, and continued to sweep the country. But Spitamenes was not yet beaten. He persuaded the Massagetae to help him, overwhelmed one of the border forts of Bactria, and a few days later appeared before Bactra itself, behind Alexander's back. The king had left Craterus with a strong force to patrol Bactria and prevent a rising, but in Bactra there were only details and the sick. The commandant of the hospital led them out; Spitamenes ambushed and annihilated them. Craterus came up in haste, but Spitamenes escaped into the desert with little loss. It had taken Alexander half the campaigning season of 328 to reduce about half of Sogdiana, and still Spitamenes was at large; but the country was now a network of fortified posts and garrisons. He left Coenus in charge of western Sogdiana with two battalions of the phalanx, two squadrons of the Companions, and the newly raised Bactrian and Sogdian horse, the first Asiatic troops in his army; he himself made his headquarters at Nautaka, possibly to rest what troops he could for the winter campaign and attend to administration, but there is some confusion here in the chronology.[1] Spitamenes was sadly hampered by the

---

1 Arr. IV, 18, 2, he rests the army at Nautaka, it being mid-winter; as soon as spring appears, 18, 4, he attacks the strongholds of Oxyartes ånd Chorienes; there is some snow at the first, but at the second much more snow falls and the army suffers from cold, 21, 10. He returns to Bactra, and starts for India at the end of spring, 22, 3, ἐξήκοντος τοῦ ἦρος. On this scheme it is impossible to get in all that happened at Bactra before he

fortified posts, but by the promise of plunder he roused the Massagetae to another effort; they gave him 3,000 horse, and with these and his own Sogdians he attacked Coenus. But Coenus had mastered his tactics, and he too had light horse. Spitamenes was decisively defeated, and his Sogdians left him and surrendered; the Massagetae lost heart, cut off his head, and sent it to Alexander. He was the best opponent Alexander met. His blood was continued in the line of the Seleucid kings; for Alexander subsequently married his daughter Apama to Seleucus, and she became the mother of Antiochus I.

This same summer saw the murder of Cleitus the Black at Maracanda.[1] The dry climate of Turkestan, and the bad water, induced in the army much use of strong native wine. Alexander himself, as is quite clear, habitually drank no more than other Macedonians;[2] he sat long at dinner, but chiefly for the sake of conversation; the stories of his excessive drinking were first put about after his death by Ephippus of Olynthus, a scurrilous gossip-monger[3] who was not with the army, and were afterwards spread by the New Comedy. However, at this particular banquet Alexander did get drunk, as did Cleitus; but the conversation in which the quarrel originated cannot be

finally quitted it; he must have taken the two strongholds by mid-winter, and the army's rest at Bactra *after* they were taken has become transferred to some temporary halt at Nautaka *before* they were taken.

1 Curtius VIII, 1, 19 says Maracanda; he often uses Ptolemy. Arrian (IV, 8, 1) *implies* Bactra; but some time in early summer 328 is certain (Arr. ibid. a little while after Alexander left Bactra to invade Sogdiana the second time) and Alexander did not take the army back across the Oxus, while all the columns did unite at Maracanda.

2 Aristobulus, fr. 62 (48), Jacoby = Arr. VII, 29, 4. See § D, p. 41 and n. 5.

3 See App. 22, I, p. 354, n. 2.

reconstructed with any certainty from the varying versions. It seems probable that some Greek recited a sarcastic poem about the Macedonian officers defeated by Spitamenes, and that in some way Parmenion's name was brought up, probably with a suggestion of failure; Cleitus, who had been Philotas' principal lieutenant, thought Alexander approved, and began to defend Parmenion and Philip's men generally, and went on to compare Philip with Alexander, whose Persian innovations he was known to dislike. Alexander became angry, possibly at being belittled, but possibly too at the indecency of such a comparison; Cleitus, too drunk to understand, went on to assert that Alexander owed his victories to Philip's Macedonians. What he seems to have been trying to express was that Alexander was slighting the men whose bravery alone had raised him to a position in which he *could* slight them. Alexander made some effort at self-control; he turned to two Greeks beside him and said 'Don't you feel like demigods among beasts?' But Cleitus could not be restrained; he thrust out his hand towards Alexander and said 'This saved your life at the Granicus,' and continued to taunt him. Then Alexander's temper gave way utterly; he sprang up and snatched a spear from a guard, but some held him down, while Ptolemy pushed Cleitus out of the hall. He broke away, however, and hearing Alexander shouting his name rushed back, crying 'Here is Cleitus, Alexander.' Alexander ran him through on the spot.

When the king came to himself his remorse was bitter. He shut himself up for three days, taking no food, and calling on the names of Cleitus and his sister Lanice, who had been his nurse and to whom he had made such a fine return. The army became alarmed; they might be left leaderless at the end of the earth. At last his friends persuaded him to eat; the soothsayers gave out that Cleitus' death was due to the anger of Dionysus for a neglected sacrifice, and the army passed a resolution that Cleitus had been justly executed. The philosopher Anaxarchus is said to have told Alexander roughly not to be a fool: kings could do no wrong. One hopes it is not true, though Aristotle had said much the same: when the supreme ruler did come, he would be above all laws.[1] But he had meant human laws. Terrible as the incident seems to us, it probably affected the generals very little; life was cheap and you took your chances; Cleitus (as Aristobulus says)[2] had only himself to thank. Arrian's kindly verdict is, that many kings had done evil, but he had never heard of another who repented.[3]

While at Nautaka Alexander removed Autophradates from Tapuria and added it to Phrataphernes' satrapy, and restored Darius' former satrap Atropates to Media; these two men were loyal to him throughout, as they had been to Darius. Artabazus was permitted to retire on account of his age, and a Macedonian, another Amyntas, was made satrap of Bactria and Sogdiana; it was obviously an impossible post for any Persian. But Alexander had not yet conquered all Sogdiana. He held the plain country; but four great barons, Oxyartes, Chorienes, Catanes, and Austanes, were still in arms in the hills of Paraetacene. Late in 328 Alexander attacked Oxyartes' stronghold, the 'Sogdian rock', perhaps near Derbent; Oxyartes was not

1 Arist. *Pol.* III, 13, 1284a, 10–13. On this, the 'god among men' passage, see App. 22, II, pp. 366 sqq.
2 Aristobulus, fr. 29 (23), Jacoby = Arr. IV, 8, 9.
3 Arr. VII, 29, 1; cf. IV, 9, 6.

there, but his family was. The snow was so deep, and the rock so precipitous, that the garrison told Alexander he would never take it unless he found men who could fly. Alexander called for volunteers; 300 answered and went up with ropes and iron pegs; 30 fell and were killed, but the rest climbed the crag overlooking the fortress and hoisted the agreed signal. Alexander told the garrison to go and look at his flying men, whereon they surrendered. Among the captives was Oxyartes' daughter Roxane, whom Alexander married. It was a marriage of policy, intended to reconcile the eastern barons and end the national war. Tradition naturally represents him as in love with her, but it is doubtful if he ever cared for any woman except his terrible mother. On hearing the news Oxyartes came in, and accompanied Alexander to the siege of Chorienes' stronghold, on the Vakhsh river south of Faisabad. The 'rock' was protected by a deep cañon, at the bottom of which ran the torrent; the garrison thought it could never be crossed. But Alexander set the whole army to work day and night making ladders; with these they descended the ravine on a broad front, fixed pegs in the rock, and bridged the river with hurdles covered with earth. Chorienes took fright, and Oxyartes secured his surrender by enlarging on the clemency and good faith which Alexander had shown toward the defenders of his own stronghold. Alexander then left Craterus to reduce Catanes and Austanes and the land east of the Vakhsh, which he accomplished successfully, while he himself returned to Bactra to prepare for the expedition to India. During his stay in Bactria he refounded Bactra as an Alexandria, and founded two other Alexandrias, one at Merv and one at Tarmita (Termez) on the north bank of the Oxus where the trade route to Bactra from Samarcand and the north came to the river.[1] He also arranged for the education and training in Macedonian fashion of 30,000 native youths.

At Bactra there came up the question of Alexander's divine descent.[2] The man who publicly brought it forward was the philosopher Callisthenes. He was anxious to please Alexander, as he hoped to secure from him the rebuilding of his native city Olynthus; he also had an exaggerated opinion of his own importance as the self-constituted historian of the expedition; he is reported to have said that Alexander's fame depended not on what Alexander did but on what Callisthenes wrote. Some time after 330 he had sent to Greece for publication his history of Alexander, so far as it had gone; he must have read it to Alexander and others, and it was doubtless well known. It was written to advertise Alexander, with an eye to the Greek opposition; he has been called Alexander's press agent, but that is hardly accurate, for Alexander was not making use of him; he wrote what he himself wished to write. His book contained some very extravagant inventions. He said[3] that the oracle of Apollo at Didyma, so long silent, had again spoken and declared that Alexander was the son of Zeus; that a prophetess at Erythrae had confirmed his divine origin; and that in his passage along the Pamphylian coast at Mount Climax (p. 21), the very waves had known their lord and had made *proskynesis* to him, i.e. had worshipped him as a god. But the thing that mattered most was his alteration of the greeting of the priest of Ammon; the

1 On these two cities and their subsequent history, see Tarn, *Tarmita, J.H.S.* LX, 1940, p. 89, and App. 8, 1, pp. 234 sq.
2 For what follows, see App. 22, 1.
3 Callisthenes, Jacoby, II, no. 124, fr. 14 = Strabo XVII, 1, 43 (814), and fr. 31. See App. 22, 1, pp. 357 sq.

priest had naturally greeted the new Pharaoh as son of Ammon, and Callisthenes altered this to son of Zeus. He thus brought the question of Alexander's divine son-ship into the Greek religious sphere; doubtless he thought it would please Alexander. It had a certain plausibility, for Zeus was the traditional ancestor, through Heracles, of the Argead kings; and as some must have known the story that Philip had doubted whether Alexander were really his son, the seed Callisthenes sowed fell on fertile ground, and at Bactra, if not before, the flatterers who now surrounded Alexander, notably Anaxarchus and certain poetasters,[1] were calling him son of Zeus. Up to this time there had been a clear distinction between being the son of a god and being a god; all the mortal sons of Zeus had not been raised to heaven. But by the third century B.C. the distinction had become blurred,[2] and that process was already beginning; some of the chorus of flatterers were hinting that Alexander was a god, just as Callisthenes had hinted it in his story of Mount Climax. Of Alexander's own mind we know little. He never called himself son of Ammon,[3] and to be so called by others roused him to fury, and few ever dared do it; whatever his relationship with Ammon exactly was, it was evidently to him something not for profane tongues. Equally, he never called himself son of Zeus;[4] but he allowed others so to call him. Naturally he did not believe it; he was occasionally sarcastic on the subject, and in public regularly alluded to his father Philip. But as he permitted it, he may have thought that some day it might have its uses.

In the spring of 327 the whole matter came to a head.[5]

1 See § E'.   2 App. 22, II, p. 362, n. 2.   3 App. 22, I, pp. 350, 354 sq.
4 Ibid. pp. 350, 352 sq.   5 On what follows, see App. 22, II.

Alexander had already initiated his policy of fusion, the fusion of the Macedonian and Persian elements in his empire; apart from his Persian satraps, he had, since Darius' death, adopted on State occasions Persian dress and Persian court ceremonial, and had made Chares the historian chamberlain. He now resolved to introduce the Persian custom of prostration (*proskynesis*) for all those approaching the king. To Persians it was only a ceremony; the Achaemenid kings had not been gods, and prostration in Persian eyes did not imply worship. But to Greeks and Macedonians it did imply worship; man did not prostrate himself save to the gods. Alexander knew perfectly how Greeks must interpret prostration, and must therefore have intended to become a god; and as Greeks, Macedonians, and Persians were all involved, it can only mean that he intended to become, officially, the god of his empire; he was doing rather more than feeling his way. His reasons were entirely political; the thing was to him merely a pretence which might form a useful instrument of state-craft and become, he thought, a considerable help to his policy of fusion; also, among other things, he had to settle how the autocrat of Asia, without playing the autocrat, could get a juridical standing in those free Greek cities in whose hands lay his empire's access to the Aegean. What put the idea of becoming a god into his head seems clear enough. It had been put there, long before he crossed to Asia, by the two chief political thinkers of his youth, his tutor Aristotle and Isocrates; for Isocrates had said to Philip that, if he conquered Persia, nothing would be left him but to become a god,[1] and Aristotle, not content with

1 Isoc. *Ep.* 3.

telling Alexander that he had no peer,[1] had said, with Alexander in mind, that the supreme ruler when he came would be as a god among men.[2] Whether Callisthenes really had much to do with it, as some believed later, can hardly be said; he may perhaps have been one of the factors which led Alexander to believe that the time was ripe.

Such was the background of Alexander's attempt to introduce *proskynesis*. He had the support of Hephaestion and one or two other Macedonians; and both he and Hephaestion believed that Callisthenes would aid them, as was natural after his story of the sea prostrating itself before the king; some indeed asserted that Callisthenes had promised. But when prostration was actually introduced, events took an unexpected course. The Macedonians offered no actual opposition, but their displeasure and even anger were evident; one general did worse than oppose— he laughed. But the first Greek called on, Callisthenes, opposed in good earnest and asked Alexander to confine this Asiatic custom to Asiatics. Alexander had a strong sense of what was possible; he dropped prostration for good and all, and with it the idea of becoming the god of his Empire. But he was furious with Callisthenes. He had counted on his influence as an aid to his policy, and Callisthenes had failed him.

The reason for Callisthenes' change of attitude has been debated ever since, without much result.[3] In the Peripatetic literature drawn on by Plutarch in his *Life* of Alexander he

1 Arist. fr. 659 (if true): σοὶ δὲ οὐδεὶς ἴσος.
2 Arist. *Pol.* III, 13, 1284*a*, 10-13, on which see App. 22, II, pp. 366 sqq.
3 It has even led to a suggestion, which has found no acceptance, that the '*Acts of Alexander*' cannot have been written by Callisthenes the philosopher; P. Corssen, *Philol.* LXXIV, 1917, p. 1.

figures as a lover of liberty opposing a tyrant;[1] he was of course the same Callisthenes, the man who, Aristotle said, had no sense.[2] Doubtless, as Aristotle's pupil, he despised barbarians and objected to Persian ceremonial; but the time to think of that was before he wrote about Mount Climax, and hinted that Alexander was a god. To say that he had Panhellenic ideas, and wished to make of Alexander a god for Greeks but not for Persians, is no explanation, for to make Alexander actually a god at all was not his intention; he had merely been playing with fire, with the usual result. One may suppose that he had only meant to write up Alexander in extravagant terms, and suddenly found himself (as he thought) faced with the terrible consequences of what he had done; the god he had helped to make meant to act as such; it was no longer rhetoric but sober earnest. He tried to draw back, too late.

Then came the Pages' conspiracy. One of the royal pages, Hermolaus, had anticipated Alexander at a boar-hunt; he was deprived of his horse and whipped, apparently the usual Macedonian custom.[3] He and some friends thereon conspired to kill Alexander; they were detected and put to death. This act of personal revenge had no political import, but it involved Callisthenes, who had been Hermolaus' tutor. Whether he was formally a party to the conspiracy is uncertain; but he had indulged in some wild talk to the boys on the virtue of killing tyrants, and Ptolemy says the boys confessed that this talk lay at the bottom of the whole business. Alexander put Callisthenes to death,

---

1 As the worthless Demades subsequently became a martyred hero; Crönert, *Anzeiger Akad. Wien*, 1924, No. VIII, on Berlin Papyrus 13045.
2 Plut. *Alex.* LIV, νοῦν οὐκ εἶχεν. Cf. Jacoby II, no. 124, T. 5.
3 Given in the collection of Macedonian customs used by Curtius (VIII, 8, 3); see § G, pp. 106 sq.

presumably for conspiracy; to relieve him of odium, Chares spread a story that Callisthenes died naturally in prison.[1] The verdict of the historian Timaeus may be recorded: Callisthenes deserved his fate, for he had made of a man a god, and done all in his power to destroy Alexander's soul.[2] How far the verdict is true will probably never be known. But Callisthenes had his revenge; and Alexander paid. He incurred the hostility of Aristotle's school; Theophrastus in a pamphlet[3] lamented Callisthenes' death and branded Alexander as a tyrant, and Demetrius of Phalerum presently carried the school over to Alexander's enemy Cassander; and the two philosophers worked out a doctrine of Chance, which was applied to Alexander.[4] Thus from the Peripatetic school, of which Callisthenes had been a member, arose that debased portrait of Alexander[5] against which Plutarch so passionately protested,[6] and from which history for long could not shake itself free—the portrait of a despot whose achievements were due to luck, and who was ruined at the end by the excess of his own fortune.

Alexander received large reinforcements while in Bactria, and reorganised his army for the invasion of India. The phalanx[7] was raised from six to seven battalions, Antipater,

1 Chares, Jacoby II, no. 125, fr. 15, and many later writers; see Jacoby, Kallisthenes, no. 124, T. 17, 18.
2 Timaeus in Polyb. XII, 12 b. For the interesting turn given to this in Ps.-Call. A', see App. 22, p. 365.
3 Καλλισθένης ἢ περὶ πένθους. See Jacoby II, no. 124, T. 19.
4 Demetrius: Polyb. XXIX, 21, 1–9. Theophrastus: his *Callisthenes*, see Cic. *Tusc.* III, 21.
5 The Peripatetic portrait is given at full length by Curtius; see § G, passim.
6 In *de Alexandri fortuna* I, directed against both Stoics and Peripatetics. See App. 16, p. 298; Tarn, *A.J.P.* LX, 1939, pp. 55 sq.
7 App. I, II, where the changes in the command are fully discussed.

whose hands were free after the defeat of Sparta, having sent him another battalion of seasoned troops commanded by Cleitus the White. Of the old phalanx-leaders, Craterus had now taken Parmenion's place as second in command, Perdiccas was a Bodyguard, and Amyntas dead; Coenus, Polyperchon, and Meleager remained, but Coenus' defeat of Spitamenes had marked him for early promotion; new men appear, and there were to be further changes in India. The hypaspists,[1] now commanded by Seleucus, the future king, were unaltered; Nearchus had an interim command of one of the battalions. Alexander also took with him, besides the indispensable Agrianians, the Thracian foot and Balacrus' javelin-men (if they were not the same corps), and an enlarged archer force, with a corps of slingers, but very few mercenaries; he had been leaving mercenaries in every satrapy and newly-founded city, and of necessity he left a large force of them, 3,500 horse and 10,000 foot (who probably included what remained of the 8,000 mercenaries of Issus) with the satrap Amyntas in Bactria. If every formation was again at paper strength, and taking the highest possible figures, he might have had 20,000–22,000 foot,[2] all Europeans.

There were great changes in the cavalry.[3] Hephaestion still commanded his hipparchy of the Companions, four squadrons; but after the death of Cleitus the Black Alexander had taken command of the other hipparchy himself, one of its four squadrons being the Royal squadron, henceforth always called the *agēma* (Guard), which thus came under his personal command; this enabled him to incorporate in it the sons of a few great Persian nobles, and it was now raised to 300 men, if indeed it had not been so

1 App. 1, III.   2 See App. 1, v, p. 169.   3 For what follows see App. 1, IV.

all the time. The Companions themselves had come back again to 1,700, the establishment figure of 200 to a squadron (2 *lochoi*) with the *agēma* of 300. Alexander kept them with him, but sent home all his Balkan cavalry except the Thracians in Media with Cleander, who had taken Parmenion's place as general of that sector of communications. In their stead, as became the Great King, he was recruiting his own subjects, the Eastern Iranian horse who had fought him hard and now served him well. After his final reorganisation at Taxila (pp. 92–3), he had (paper strength) 6,300 horse, plus a few mercenaries. This meant that he invaded India with an army of from 27,000 to 30,000 men, if every corps was up to paper strength; any figure over 30,000 is impossible, and it cannot be asserted that every corps was up to paper strength. It was thus a smaller force than that with which he had crossed the Dardanelles; for a time he had managed to keep his European field army at a fairly constant figure, but now he had to rely more and more on Asiatics. Plutarch's story[1] that his army in India numbered 120,000 foot and 15,000 horse is, as it stands, ridiculous; but if there be reckoned in the native 'wives' and children of the soldiery, the technicians and writers, the traders and camp-followers, the auxiliary services, the seamen, and the contingents and retinues of the Indian princes, there must have been a very large number of people in camp on the Jhelum. The army had become a moving State,[2] a reflection of the Empire; and provision was made for training the soldiers' children.

1 Plut. *Alex.* LXVI, invented for the sake of the propaganda statement that three-quarters of them were lost in Gedrosia; this shows that the inventor had in mind an army of 30,000 foot and 3,750 horse. Repeated, Arr. *Ind.* 19, 5 (not from Nearchus).
2 On such armies see M. Rostovtzeff, *Soc. and Econ. Hist.* pp. 143–7.

To understand Alexander's invasion of India we must discard all ideas later than 327 and try to see 'India' as he then saw it.[1] He never knew of the existence of northern or eastern Asia—of Siberia and Chinese Turkestan, China and further India; to the end of his life, 'Asia' meant to him, as to everyone, the empire of Darius I. He knew nothing of the Ganges (unless perhaps the name)[2] or of eastern Hindustan, which were unknown to Greeks prior to Megasthenes, or of the Indian peninsula, though later Nearchus and Onesicritus collected dim reports of 'islands' further south. There is no evidence that he even knew of the Rajputana desert, which Herodotus had known. 'India' to Alexander, when he invaded it, meant the country of the Indus, which, following Aristotle, he thought was a broad-based peninsula jutting *eastward* into the sea from the land mass of Iran. Along the north side of it, like a backbone, ran a chain of mountains, Aristotle's 'Parnasos' (i.e. Paropanisus); the rest was a plain, traversed by the Indus and its tributaries. Ocean, which was near the Jaxartes, washed the northern base of these mountains, and flowed round the eastern end of the peninsula. As to the south side, he began by sharing the perplexities of Aristotle, who at one time thought, like Aeschylus,[3] that 'India' had land connection with Ethiopia (making the Indian Ocean a lake), and at another believed that the sea separated them.

'India' had once been fairly well-known. Darius I had ruled the Paropamisadae and Gandhāra, and had subsequently conquered Sind and probably further parts of the

1 He brought Aristotle's views with him; for these, as here given, see Aristot. *Meteor.* I, 13, p. 350*a*, 18, and the *Liber de inundacione Nili.*
2 See App. 14.
3 Aesch. *Supp.* 284-6; cf. Damastes in Strabo I, 3, I (47).

Punjab; his admiral Scylax was said to have sailed down the Indus and back to Egypt, and though the truth of this has been doubted, Darius may have made some use of the Indian Ocean.[1] The idea of the earliest Indian punch-marked silver coinage had perhaps been suggested by the Achaemenid coinage;[2] the official Aramaic writing of the Achaemenids had been introduced in Gandhāra and at Taxila (Takshaçilā), to become the parent of the Kharoshthī script.[3] Taxila itself contained an Iranian element, among whom Zoroastrian customs prevailed.[4] But the fourth century had forgotten these things. To Ephorus, Indians were as shadowy as Celts. Herodotus was no longer much read; even Callisthenes could neglect him,[5] and there is no sign that Alexander knew him at all, not even his account of Scylax's voyage. On the Persian side, the Achaemenids had lost the satrapies of Sind, Gandhāra, and the Paropamisadae; Alexander met no Persian officials east of the Hindu Kush. Ochus had even believed that India joined Ethiopia and that the Indus was the upper Nile;[6] this theory influenced Aristotle and, through him, Alexander, who started by believing it, though he soon learnt the truth. 'India' had become dim to the West.

But 'India' had been part of the empire of Darius I; and Alexander's invasion was only the necessary and inevitable completion of his conquest of that empire. It had nothing to do with any scheme of world-conquest; indeed it could

1 Herod. IV, 44, ἐχρᾶτο. See *C.A.H.* IV, p. 200.
2 J. Allan, *B.M. Coin Catalogue: Ancient India*, 1936, p. lxxi.
3 See Tarn, *Bactria and India*, p. 162.
4 Besides Aristobulus, fr. 42, Jacoby = Strabo xv, 1, 62 (714), see Tarn, op. cit. p. 137, n. 3.
5 For a glaring instance, see App. 13.
6 From Aristotle's *Liber de inundacione Nili*.

not have, for in the far East the 'world', like 'Asia', only meant the Persian empire; nothing else was known. Possibly Alexander did not know, any more than we do, exactly how much of the Punjab Darius I had ruled; on the other hand, with his known interest in Cyrus, he possibly believed Xenophon's mistaken statement that Cyrus had ruled all 'India' to the eastern ocean;[1] in either case he naturally meant to reduce the entire province, like any other satrapy. He had already, while at Bactra, formed some political connections there; a chief from Gandhāra, Sasigupta, who had helped Bessus, had come over to him, and he had been promised aid by the powerful rajah of Taxila, who was having difficulty in withstanding his neighbour Porus and turned naturally to the new King of Persia, whose forerunners had once been Taxila's suzerains. Incidentally, Alexander greatly desired, as did Aristotle, to solve the problem of Ocean and the relationship of 'India' to Egypt. He meant therefore to explore the southern sea with a fleet; for this purpose he took with him to India rowers and shipwrights from Phoenicia, Cyprus, Caria, and Egypt, and had already decided that his friend Nearchus should be admiral. That is why Nearchus was recalled from his satrapy and given an interim command in the hypaspists, an apparent reduction in rank which must have puzzled those not in the secret.

In early summer 327 Alexander started from Bactra. Local tradition says that he recrossed the Hindu Kush by the lofty Kaoshan pass, 14,300 ft. high, but doubtless he

---

1 Xen. *Cyr.* VIII, 6, 20 sq. Xenophon in saying 'east' had the points of the compass wrong; the same mistake in Herod. IV, 44, πρὸς ἠῶ. Such errors are common, e.g. Ptolemy, the geographer, put the Orkneys east of, instead of north of, Caithness; for several other instances, see Tarn, *Bactria and India*, p. 476 and n. 8.

took the usual route by Bamyan and the Ghorband valley, which turned the range (p. 66). He found Alexandria of the Caucasus in disorder; he left Nicanor as governor to organise the city, and soon after made Oxyartes satrap of Paropamisadae. On his way to the Cabul river he was met by the local chiefs and the new ruler of Taxila, Ambhi (officially called Taxiles), the son of the old rajah, who was dead. They gave Alexander 25 elephants which they had with them (he did not, however, use elephants except for transport), and Taxiles put himself and his kingdom at his disposal. There Alexander divided his army, and sent Hephaestion and Perdiccas with Taxiles and the baggage and part of the army through the Khyber pass to the Indus, with orders to build a bridge of boats; he himself with his four squadrons of the Companions, four battalions of the phalanx, the hypaspists, archers, Agrianians, horse-javelin men, and the siege-train, intended to march through the hills to the north of the Cabul river, to secure Hephaestion's northern flank from attack, his southern flank being protected by the nature of the ground.

Breaking camp about November, Alexander followed the old route through Laghman, ascended the Kunar river, and crossed into Bajaur, whose warlike people the Greeks called Aspasii. He attempted to prevent their concentration by the speed of his movements; he had much hard local fighting, was again wounded, and took several towns, including the capital Arigaion (Bajaur); but he could not prevent the tribes concentrating for battle. He attacked their army in three columns, led by Ptolemy, Leonnatus, and himself, and after a severe fight broke them, taking many prisoners and cattle; he was so struck by the beauty of the cattle that he sent the best to Macedonia. He then left Bajaur, crossed the Landai river below the junction of the Panjkora and Swat, and entered Swat, the country of the Assaceni, who had concentrated before their capital Massaga; with them was a body of mercenaries from beyond the Indus. They did not wait to be attacked, but attacked him themselves. Alexander, who led the phalanx, feigned flight to draw them from the walls; but though he defeated them they reached the city with little loss, and in trying to rush the place he was wounded in the ankle. He brought up his siege-train, but failed to breach the walls or to enter by a bridge, as at Tyre; and the garrison held out till their chief was killed, when they surrendered upon terms. The Indian mercenaries left the town and camped outside; in the night Alexander surrounded them and cut them to pieces. The official explanation was that they had agreed to enter his service and were meditating desertion and he found it out. The explanation is unsatisfactory, for it omits the real point: had they taken the oath to Alexander or not? If they had, and were really meditating desertion, he was within his rights, though the death of the ringleaders might have sufficed. If they had not, it was massacre. Probably they had not, or the official explanation must have said so; the thing may have been some horrible mistake due perhaps to defective interpreting and to Alexander's growing impatience.

It was in Swat, in the district of the Kamdesh Kafirs, near Meros (the triple-peaked mountain Koh-i-Mor), that he found a town which the Greeks called Nysa, inhabited by people who, like their modern descendants, did not re-semble the surrounding tribes; they worshipped some god (? Śiva) who could be identified with Dionysus, especially as the ivy growing on the mountain made the Macedonians home-sick. Alexander welcomed the identification, for to suppose that Dionysus had been there and that he was going farther than the god encouraged the army;[1] and he declared the Nysaeans, who probably really were immigrants from the west,[2] independent of his satrap. Before leaving Swat he took and garrisoned two other towns, Ora and Bazira,[3] and then came down through the Shāhkōt pass into the Yusufzai country (the Greek Peucelaïtis), which Hephaestion had failed to reduce; he pacified it and received the surrender of the capital Pushkalāvatī,[4] which was to be a Greek centre in the second century. He made Nicanor satrap of Gandhāra, which then meant the country between the Kunar river and the Indus, and next halted at a place called Embolima (unidentified), two days from a mountain called by the Greeks Aornos, on which many Indians had found refuge. Heracles (Krishna) was said to have failed to take it, and Alexander decided to do so. He left Craterus with much of the army at Embolima, to support and supply him should a siege be necessary, and went on with some selected troops.

Aornos, long sought in vain, has now been identified[5] in

1 See § E, p. 46.
2 They were one of the foreign peoples, Iranians or others, who had come in through the passes and who were classed together by Indians as Bāhlīkas (Bactrians); Tarn, *Bactria and India*, p. 169.
3 Identified as Udegram and Birkot: Sir A. Stein, *On Alexander's track to the Indus*, 1929, chaps. v and viii.
4 Later Greek Peucela: Tarn, op. cit. p. 237, nn. 4, 5. Arrian, in *Anab.* iv, 28, 6 and *Ind.* 1, 1, 8, has given the town the name of the later eparchy, Peucelaïtis.
   By Sir A. Stein; see *On Alexander's track to the Indus*, chaps. xvi–xxi. Arrian, who is following Ptolemy, never mentions the ravine, though he describes the building of the ramp and the consequential operations; presumably something has fallen out of the text towards the end of iv, 29, 6. The accounts in Diodorus and Curtius are both partly fanciful, though Curtius has used Ptolemy to some extent.

the mountains north of the Buner river, near the Indus. Two high ridges of over 7,000 ft., Pīr-sar, which is broad at the top, and Ūṇa-sar, meet at right angles, forming a position shaped like an inverted capital L; Ūṇa-sar could be equated philologically with the Greek Aornos.[1] The actual 'rock', the cone of Bar-sar, is at the end of Pīr-sar, separated from Ūṇa-sar by the steep Būrimār ravine. Alexander sent Ptolemy with the light-armed troops, some picked hypaspists, and an Indian guide by a track up Ūṇa-sar; they reached the summit unmarked and palisaded a camp. The same day Alexander, who had Coenus' battalion of the phalanx, some picked men from the other battalions, presumably some hypaspists, and the catapults,[2] attempted Pīr-sar, his plan being a converging attack on Bar-sar along both ridges (he did not know of the Būrimār ravine), but the ascent was difficult and he was beaten back; the Indians then attacked Ptolemy's camp, but were repulsed. Next day Alexander fought his way up Ūṇa-sar and joined Ptolemy, and the combined forces advanced along the ridge towards Bar-sar, to find themselves blocked by the ravine, 600 ft. deep and 500 yd. across. Alexander began building a ramp across it with tree-trunks and earth, getting his catapults and slingers out on to the ramp as it grew; some Macedonians got across and seized a position on the far side, and when the ramp was completed the Indians gave up, and Alexander stormed the 'rock' as they fled. He left Sasigupta to hold it.

From Aornos he pursued a chief still in arms through Swat to Dyrta, presumably somewhere in Buner;[3] the man

---

1 Stein, op. cit. p. 152.
2 Only the essential parts were usually carried, the wooden framework being built on the spot as required. 3 Stein, op. cit. p. 158.

escaped, but Alexander captured his elephants. He then joined Hephaestion on the Indus. Hephaestion had bridged the river at Ohind, 16 miles above Attock, and had built in sections a number of boats, including some triakontors (light warships of 15 oars a side); while Taxiles had sent 30 elephants. Alexander crossed the Indus in early spring 326, and at Taxila, now excavated,[1] his army for the first time saw a great Indian city. It was both a commercial centre and a famous university town, a headquarters of the teaching of the Brahmans. Taxiles gave Alexander 56 more elephants and some information. He was at war with the Paurava king (Porus), whose country lay in the plains between the Hydaspes (Jhelum) and the Acesines (Chenab), and who had allied himself with Abisares, ruler of the hill states of Rajauri and Bimber, both now included in Kashmir. Porus, however, had himself an enemy beyond the Chenab, the 'free nations' or Aratta (kingless ones), who were too strong for him to conquer; these peoples, the Cathaei, Oxydracae, and Malli, were confederations of village communities under oligarchic rule.

Alexander made Taxila his advanced base for the invasion of the Punjab, and while there reorganised his cavalry.[2] He separated the *agēma* altogether from the Companions and kept it under his personal command, and of the rest (except the horse-archers and the few mercenaries he had) he made five hipparchies, each of 1,000 men. The first four contained one squadron apiece of the Companions, 300 strong, and were filled up with Eastern

---

1 An account of Sir J. Marshall's excavations year by year has been given in the *Archaeological Survey of India* from 1912–13 onwards; see also his *Guide to Taxila*[2] and his forthcoming work on Taxila.

2 App. 1, IV, pp. 164 sqq.

Iranian horse, who, however, did not become Companions, but were regarded merely as brigaded with them; the four hipparchs were Hephaestion, Perdiccas, Craterus and Coenus. The fifth hipparchy, commanded by Demetrius, a promoted squadron-leader of the Companions, was chiefly Iranian, but contained what few Companions were left over. Coenus' promotion left vacant his battalion of the phalanx, which was given to his son Antigenes[1] but, as was not unusual, continued sometimes to be called by the name of its old commander; it had been the crack battalion, specially picked for the attacks at Tyre and Aornos. The other six phalanx-leaders were now Meleager, Polyperchon, Perdiccas' brother Alcetas, Amyntas' brother Attalus, Gorgias, and Cleitus the White. Alexander left a garrison in Taxila, made Harpalus' brother Philippus satrap, and advanced to the Hydaspes at Jhelum,[2] which he probably reached early in June.

The river was not yet at its full size, but the rains would soon begin; and Porus with his army, including many elephants, held the farther bank. Alexander had the flotilla from the Indus brought across in sections, and made ostentatious preparations for crossing to hold Porus' attention, though he knew that the cavalry could not cross in face of the elephants. Under cover of these preparations he reconnoitred the bank, and selected a place 18 miles above[3] Jhelum, at the great bend of the river, where was a wooded island in mid-stream. The rains had begun, and there was need of haste. The boats were brought to the selected point

1 For the relationship, see App. 17, p. 314.
2 Whether Alexander's camp was at Jhelum or Jalalpur has been disputed for a century; see App. 6, pp. 197 sq.
3 Frontinus 1, 4, 9 proves that the crossing was made *above* Porus' camp.

and put together; meanwhile Alexander made numerous feints at crossing elsewhere, keeping Porus perpetually on the move; the Indian finally grew weary of meeting threats that never materialised. Shortly after the summer solstice, Alexander joined his flotilla by a wide detour, leaving Craterus at Jhelum with his hipparchy, two battalions of the phalanx (those of Alcetas and Polyperchon), and the Indian contingents from Gandhāra, who, however, took no part in the battle; his orders were not to cross unless Porus were defeated or the elephants withdrawn from the bank. To guard against a surprise crossing, three battalions of the phalanx, those of Meleager, Attalus, and Gorgias, were strung out along the bank between Jhelum and the crossing-point; their orders[1] were to cross in turn and join Alexander as he successively came level with them on his march towards Porus' camp. The following night was exceptionally stormy.

Alexander had with him the *agēma* of the Companions, the hipparchies of Hephaestion, Perdiccas, Coenus, and Demetrius, and the horse-archers, nominally 5,300 horse. Of infantry he had the hypaspists, two battalions of the phalanx, those of Coenus (Antigenes) and Cleitus, the Agrianians, archers and javelin-men, somewhere about 10,000 men. Ptolemy's statement (if it be his) that he had under 6,000 foot is, for once, demonstrably wrong;[2] if taken from the *Journal*, it was given there simply with the object of minimising the effect of the enemy's elephants. In the morning the force crossed to the island; but as soon as they left it they were seen by Porus' scouts. They landed safely, only to find themselves on another island; with

---

1 App. 6, p. 190. See this Appendix for the problems in Arrian's account of this battle.   2 App. 6, p. 192.

great difficulty they waded ashore, and Alexander at once advanced downstream towards Porus' position, on the way defeating and killing Porus' son, who had been sent forward with 2,000 horse to reconnoitre. Porus himself, leaving a few elephants to prevent Craterus crossing, had followed, and drew up his army at right angles to the river; his left, however, did not rest on the river, but gave ample space for cavalry to manoeuvre. As Alexander was superior in cavalry, Porus' reason is obscure, unless it was to obtain drier ground for his archers. His centre was formed by 200 elephants; behind and between them the infantry were drawn up, with a body of infantry on each wing unprotected by elephants. His best infantry, the archers, carried huge bows capable of shooting a long arrow with great force; but one end of the bow had to be rested on the ground, and the slippery mud handicapped them badly. On either flank were his cavalry, some 3,000–4,000 altogether.

The battle with Porus differs from Alexander's other battles in that he could neither win with his cavalry nor help his infantry, since his horses would not approach the elephants; all he could do was to prevent Porus' cavalry, whose horses were trained to elephants, from interfering while the infantry fought it out. He had his heavy infantry in line, with the light-armed on either flank, Seleucus leading the hypaspists and Antigenes the five battalions of the phalanx; he himself with all the cavalry was on the extreme right. Out of bowshot he halted, to breathe the infantry; and Porus, seeing the massed cavalry, brought all his own cavalry round to his left. Alexander began by sending his horse-archers to attack the infantry of Porus' left wing outside the elephants and keep them occupied; his own infantry had orders not to attack till he had defeated

Porus' cavalry. He had to draw that cavalry away from the elephants; he therefore ordered Coenus to take two hipparchies and move off as if toward Porus' right (Alexander's left); then, when the Indian cavalry, seeing the force opposed to them, should charge, his orders were to take them in rear.[1] If Alexander knew that the Indian cavalry, a weaker force than his own, would charge him, this could only be because he intended to make them do so; the inducement was the division of his force; they would imagine Coenus was going to support the horse-archers, and would see only two hipparchies with Alexander. The plan worked; the Indians attacked Alexander's two hipparchies, and while Alexander met them Coenus swung round and took them in the rear; after a sharp fight they were driven to take refuge behind the elephants. Then the Macedonian line advanced and the elephants attacked them. There was a terrific struggle, but at last the Macedonians won; many elephants were killed, the wounded broke back, and the battle was over. The pursuit was taken up by Craterus, who had crossed the river. Porus, who had fought to the last and was wounded, rode leisurely off on his huge elephant; when finally he surrendered, and Alexander asked him how he would be treated, he replied 'Like a king.' Alexander's losses were carefully concealed, but there is a conclusive proof of the desperate nature of the battle with the elephants—its effect on the minds of the generals (as seen later) and especially on that of Seleucus, who had actually fought with them; when king, he ceded whole provinces in order to obtain enough war-elephants, and they became the special arm and symbol of his dynasty.

Alexander after his victory founded two cities,[2] Alex-

.[1] App. 6, pp. 194 sqq.   [2] App. 8, 1, pp. 236 sq., 243.

andria Nicaea where his camp had stood, and Alexandria
Bucephala on the battlefield, nicknamed from his horse
which died there; and later a coin was struck to com-
memorate the battle, showing Alexander pursuing Porus'
elephant.[1] Porus became his ally, a protected native ruler;
Alexander reconciled him to Taxiles, and greatly enlarged
his kingdom. He had already enlarged Taxiles' kingdom,
which now stretched to the Jhelum, and relieved him of
subjection to Philippus; he meant the two rajahs to balance
each other. Abisares, who had not helped his ally, sent
envoys and 40 elephants to Alexander, who threatened him
with invasion unless he came in person. Alexander now
decided that, after reaching the end of 'India', he would
return down the Jhelum and Indus, reducing Sind; he left
Craterus on the Jhelum with troops to secure his communications, build a fleet and finish the new cities, and
himself advanced to the Chenab, keeping near the hills to
avoid wide crossings. It was early July, with the rains at
their full and the Chenab rising; it flooded him out of his
camp, and he had some losses crossing. He left Coenus,
perhaps already ill, at the Chenab to see to his communications and to bring the transport across, sent Porus home to
recruit troops, and advanced to the Hydraotes (Ravi),
leaving garrisons along his line of route and detaching
Hephaestion southward to conquer the kingdom of Porus'
recalcitrant nephew (between Chenab and Ravi), and place
it under Porus' rule. He then crossed the Ravi and entered
the country of the Cathaeans.

The Aratta generally were regarded as the best fighters

---

1 Once unique. A second specimen, now in the British Museum, shows
that the horseman *is* Alexander. See G. F. Hill in *Brit. Mus. Quarterly*,
1926, no. 2, p. 36, and Pl. xviii *b*.

in the Punjab; and the Cathaeans had gathered for the defence of their capital Sangala (unidentified; not Sagala-Sialcot), and had formed a triple lager of wagons outside the town. Alexander attacked the lager, himself commanding on the right and Perdiccas on the left; cavalry being useless, he led the phalanx on foot. The lager was taken, but the defenders took refuge in the town; he had to build siege-machines, and ultimately stormed the place and razed it to the ground. The desperate nature of the fighting is shown by the unique admission that Alexander had 1,200 wounded, for only the seriously wounded were ever counted. Porus was ordered to garrison the country, and Alexander pushed on to the Hyphasis (Beas), which he probably struck somewhere near Gurdaspur. It is not certain if it then joined the Sutlej at all; where the Sutlej then ran is an insoluble problem.[1] Possibly the Beas had been the boundary of Darius I;[2] it would agree with what happened.

For at the Beas the army mutinied and refused to go farther. They were tired. The heat and the rains had told heavily on them,[3] and they had been shaken by the severe fighting on the Jhelum and at Sangala. Report said that across the Beas was another Aratta people (the eastern Gandaridae[4] are meant) with an unexampled number of very large and brave elephants; after their experience with Porus they had no desire to meet those elephants. But they were even more tired in mind than in body. They had understood the conquest of Persia; but now they did not

1 See App. 14, pp. 284 sq.
2 As suggested by A. V. Williams-Jackson, *Cambridge History of India*, vol. 1, p. 341. See App. 14, p. 284.
3 Strab. xv, 1, 27 (697), from Aristobulus.
4 App. 14, pp. 279 sq.

know what they were doing or where they were going; they wanted to go home.

It was a severe blow to Alexander. True, he could not have gone much farther in any case; half his army was on his communications with Taxila, and he was using Porus' troops for garrisons. But he thought there was not much farther to go; his desire still to advance with his reduced force proves that clearly enough. The intention of conquering the Prasii, i.e. the great kingdom of Magadha on the Ganges, with which he is credited in some inferior sources, is a later legend;[1] for he knew nothing of the Ganges, unless just the name, or of Magadha. Undoubtedly traders and students from the east came to Taxila; but the Achaemenids had not known of the Ganges, and any information Alexander obtained had to be filtered through two interpreters via Persian. In fact, all that he seems to have heard of, apart from the eastern Gandaridae across the Beas, was one more unnamed river to cross, presumably the Sutlej; and then came, he supposed, the end, i.e. Ocean. To turn back meant, not only failure to secure the entire province of 'India', but failure to solve the problem of Ocean, and above all to provide for the Greeks, in his continental Empire, necessary access to a new sea to replace the home sea they would long for. Once the design of reaching the eastern Ocean failed, we see Alexander giving little further thought to the Punjab, and concentrating instead on a second-best plan, the colonisation of the Persian Gulf. How much he cared is shown by this, that almost his last act when dying was to discuss Ocean with Nearchus. He would have failed of course even without the mutiny;

1 On the Ganges legend and its ramifications, see App. 14.

it was centuries too early, and Ocean was not where he thought. But it was a great dream.

Like Achilles, Alexander retired to his tent, and waited for three days for the army to change its mind; but the army was as stubborn as he. Then he took the omens for crossing, which naturally were unfavourable; he yielded to the gods, set up by the Beas twelve altars, one for each Olympian, at which, legend said, Chandragupta afterwards sacrificed, and turned back amid the acclamation of his troops. But the actual clash of wills ended in a draw. They had stopped him going forward, but they did not get their desire, an easy return home; he went back by the way he had intended to go all along, and gave them some of the hardest fighting and worst marching of their lives. But he left his arrangements in India an unfinished sketch, to be sponged off the canvas the moment he died. He formally handed over all the country between the Jhelum and the Beas to Porus as an independent king;[1] and when, in spite of his threats, Abisares still did not come to him, he accepted his excuses, confirmed him in his kingdom as a (nominally) tributary prince, and gave him authority over the neighbouring ruler of Hazāra. Clearly Alexander no longer cared what happened east of the Jhelum.

On the Jhelum he completed his half-finished fleet—80 triakontors and some smaller warships, with horse-transports, supply vessels and numerous native boats carrying food; they were organised in divisions, and the flotilla reached the imposing total of 800 or 1,000. Nearchus commanded, and in the simple straightforward Cretan, most honest of chroniclers, Alexander had the right man;

1 Arr. VI, 2, 1, evidently a formal ceremony. See App. 24, pp. 394, 398.

Onesicritus steered Alexander's ship. The expenses of equipment were borne by 33 trierarchs—24 prominent Macedonians, 8 Greeks, and one Persian. Before the start Coenus died, a loss to the army; his hipparchy was given to Cleitus. Alexander took on board his favourite troops, the hypaspists, Agrianians, Cretans, and the *agēma* of the Companions; the rest marched in three armies, Craterus on the right bank, Hephaestion with the elephants on the left, and Philippus following; they were accompanied by the contingents of the Indian princes, and a great train of women and children, camp-followers and traders. The start was made early in November 326, with the north wind. Alexander, his preparations complete, had offered a great sacrifice to all his ancestral gods and to the gods Ammon had told him to honour, to the rivers Jhelum, Chenab, and Indus, to Poseidon and all gods and goddesses of the sea, and to Ocean himself;[1] and now at the start, standing on the prow of his ship, he poured libations from a golden cup to the three rivers, to Heracles his ancestor and to Ammon his protector, and to all the gods of his worship.[2] Then his trumpets sounded; the wooded banks rang to the shouts of the rowers and the beat of oars; and the vast procession started down the Jhelum towards the sea.

Below the confluence of the Jhelum and the Chenab the armies camped, and Alexander prepared for his last important campaign, that against the Aratta people called Malli (Mahlava), who lived on the lower Ravi, between it

1 Arr. VI, 3, 1.
2 Arr. *Ind.* 18, 11. On the difficulties arising from this unique public exhibition by Alexander of his connection with Ammon (if it be true), see App. 22, p. 351, n. 5.

and the Chenab. They were said to be in arms, and con-
federate with the Oxydracae (Ksudraka), who lived across
the Ravi to the eastward; but if so they were very ill
prepared, and were not barring his road. It is, however,
possible that the Malli, though not the Oxydracae, had
been within the Persian sphere. He planned a great drive;
he was to cross the waterless Sandar-Bār to the Ravi and
work south, driving them on to Hephaestion, who was
sent forward; Ptolemy was to guard against a break-back
westward. He took his favourite troops, crossed the desert,
and surprised the first town; the men outside had not their
arms, and were simply slaughtered; the town was then
taken and no quarter given; Perdiccas took another town
and slaughtered the fugitives. But most of the Malli broke
eastward across the Ravi to join their allies; Alexander
followed, slew many, and took a town of Brahmans,
which resisted desperately; he had to mount the wall first,
and practically all the garrison were killed. Their other
cities he found empty; he sent out detachments to scour the
woods, worked round the main body, drove them back
across the Ravi, fought a battle at the ford, and shut up
some of them in a town on the west of the river (not
Multān). The town was easily taken, but the Indians retired to the citadel; the Macedonians hung back, and
Alexander snatched a storming-ladder and went up the
wall himself, followed by his shield-bearer, Peucestas, and
Leonnatus; Abreas, a corporal, mounted another ladder;
then both ladders broke, leaving Alexander and the three
on the wall. He leapt down into the citadel, and fought
single-handed with his back to the wall till the three joined
him; Abreas was killed, and Alexander was shot through
corselet and breast by a long arrow. Peucestas covered him

in front with the holy shield of Ilium and Leonnatus on one side; a tree prevented attack on the other; they kept the enemy off till the army broke in and slew every living creature there. Alexander was carried out fainting; Perdiccas cut the arrow out with his sword and he fainted again; the report went forth that he was dead. As soon as he could be moved he had himself carried on to a ship and shown to the army.

Among Alexander's campaigns this is unique in its dreadful record of mere slaughter. The explanation probably is that the army hated it; they had no wish to fight, but as they had to, they gave no quarter; they did not mean to be turned back from their way home to quell a fresh rising. Twice Alexander had to mount the wall first to get the men to follow; it was indeed time to go home. Indirectly, this, the least creditable of his campaigns, was to cost him his life, for the wound left him weakened; while it seems to have been among the Brahmans of the Punjab that the reaction started which placed Chandragupta on the throne of a united Northern India, and blotted out nearly every trace of Alexander's rule east of the Indus. For the time being both the Malli and Oxydracae formally submitted.

The progress of the flotilla down the Chenab and the Indus cannot be traced, or the places mentioned be identified, because all the rivers, more especially the Indus, have since altered their course many times. No one can say for certain where the Indus then ran; but Aristobulus records that before their arrival it had shifted its course to 'the much deeper channel to the eastward',[1] so probably it

---

1 Aristobulus fr. 35 Jacoby = Strabo, xv, 1, 19 (693), keeping the MS. reading τὸ ἕτερον, which there is no reason to doubt. See Tarn, op. cit. p. 236.

was running in the Hakra channel, like the 'lost river of Sind' of a later day, and discharging into the Ran of Cutch. Alexander built a few more ships, and ordered two Alexandrias on the Indus, one at the confluence of the Indus and the united stream of the four rivers, and another lower down, though there is nothing to show that they were ever completed; and he secured the submission of the tribes and rulers he passed, though, as among the Malli, the Brahmans were irreconcilable. At last, about the end of July 325, he reached Patala, where the Indus then bifurcated, and halted to prepare the last stage of the journey. Craterus with the baggage and siege-train, the elephants, the sick and wounded, and three battalions of the phalanx and some archers as escort, had been already sent off homeward through the Mulla pass.

Alexander's Indian satrapies may here be noticed. There were Indian peoples west of the Indus; the satrapy of Gandhāra, and parts of those of Arachosia and of Gedrosia east of the river Purali, were of Indian blood, and there were Indian peoples in the Paropamisadae, though it was more usually reckoned to Iran. Alexander made separate governments of this Indian belt,[1] excluding the Paropamisadae. Nicanor was apparently dead, killed perhaps in suppressing a revolt in Swat, and his satrapy of Gandhāra, with part of eastern Arachosia, was given to Philippus, who was related to the royal house; Eudamus with the Thracian troops was left to support him. Philippus is also called satrap of the Malli and Oxydracae; he seems to have been intended to represent Alexander's authority generally in the north-west, east of the Kunar river, the boundary of

---

[1] Eratosthenes in Strabo, xv, 2, 9 (724).

the Paropamisadae, which was a separate satrapy. South of his satrapy, another Peithon (not the Bodyguard) was satrap of the rest of the Arachosian belt, and of the Indus valley and Sind as far as the sea. The Indian belt west of the Indus was thus divided between two satrapies; its western boundary, put very roughly, started with the Kunar river, followed the watershed to somewhere near Quetta, and ran by Kalat and the river Purali to the sea; this was the territory which Seleucus later ceded to Chandra-gupta.[1]

At Patala Alexander began to build a great harbour and docks, to secure sea connection with the west; he also explored the two arms of the Indus. The coast of the Delta probably then ran a good deal north of its present line, and the Ran of Cutch was an estuary. He first sailed down the western arm, where the fleet was caught by the bore, the dangerous tidal wave that runs up some Indian rivers. Naturally alarm was caused, and some ships were de-stroyed; but he mastered the nature of the phenomenon, sacrificed as Ammon had taught him, and sailed out into the Indian Ocean; there he sacrificed and poured a libation to Poseidon and flung his golden cup into the waves, praying that the sea might bring Nearchus and the fleet safely home. He then explored the eastern arm to lake Samārah, ascertained there was no bore, and began to build a harbour on the lake as a starting-point for Nearchus. Nearchus, for his voyage to the Persian Gulf, took the triakontors that remained and some smaller vessels, perhaps 100–150 ships. The crews would be some 3,000–5,000 men; he carried a few archers and mercenaries, and some cata-

1 Details in Tarn, op. cit. p. 100.

pults to cover a landing. He had no supply-ships; the fleet could carry food for ten days only,[1] and water at a pinch for five,[2] but practically he had to land daily for water. There was no question of the *possibility* of reaching the Gulf, and his instructions[3] were entirely practical, framed with a view to establishing regular communication by sea between Indus and Euphrates: he was to examine the beaches, harbours, islands, and water-supply along the coast, explore any gulfs, find out if there were any cities, and report what land was fertile and what barren. In September 325 he dropped down the eastern arm of the Indus to its mouth. He was timed to start with the N.E. monsoon (late October); but the local tribes were so threatening that late in September he put to sea, cutting through the sand-bar at the mouth. He met contrary winds, and was delayed 24 days at 'Alexander's harbour' (Kurachi), till he got the monsoon.

In September Alexander started for his famous march through southern Gedrosia (the Makran). He had with him the hypaspists, Agrianians, the rest of the archers, and four battalions of the phalanx; the mercenaries, horse and foot; the *agēma* of the Companions, the Macedonian squadron from each·hipparchy, and the horse-archers, the other native cavalry being sent home. There was nothing foolhardy about it. His object was to support the fleet, which was not self-supporting, by digging wells and forming depots of provisions; he knew the difficulties, but counted on an increased water-supply after the summer rains. Crossing the Arabis (Hab), he received the submission of the Oreitae of Las Bela, an Iranian people with

1 Arr. *Ind.* 23, 7.   2 Ibid. 40, 11.   3 Ibid. 32, 11.

some Indian customs, founded an Alexandria at their capital Ora,[1] and made Apollophanes satrap, with orders to collect and forward supplies from that fertile district; with him he left Leonnatus with a strong force, including the Agrianians, part of the archers, the mercenaries, horse and foot, and some cavalry, presumably the horse-archers, to complete the city and its harbour (Cocala). He himself returned to the coast and formed a depot at Cocala. As soon as he left, the Oreitae rose; Leonnatus defeated them, but Apollophanes was killed, and consequently no provisions were forwarded, which upset Alexander's arrangements. He had with him when he left Cocala perhaps some 8,000–10,000 fighting men,[2] all Macedonians (unless the archers), beside women, children, traders, and camp followers. At first he followed the coast; provisions were not plentiful, and, though he tried to form another depot, his troops broke his seals and ate the food. But the real trouble began at the river Tomeros (Hingol). He did not know of the Taloi range; it compelled him to leave the coast and strike inland. The guides lost themselves, and 200 miles of suffering in that desolate country followed. They marched only by night, because of the heat; they ate the baggage-animals and burnt the carts for firewood; all who straggled died. Alexander displayed his greatest qualities as a leader; he sent back his horse and went on foot, and refused water when there was not enough for all. He lost his personal baggage; the hardships endured are illustrated by the disorganisation of his surveying section.

1 See for all details App. 8, II, *Alexandria in Makarene.*
2 Assuming 500 archers (they had been divided between Craterus, Leonnatus, Nearchus, and Alexander), the paper total would be something over 11,000; but Alexander had had heavy (unknown) losses in India and had received no reinforcements.

At last he reached the sea at Pasni, and found enough water, and from Gwadur got the regular route to the royal residence, Pura, where he was able to rest his men. He had extricated the army without much loss, but the mortality among the non-combatants was severe. From Pura he followed the Bampur and Halil Rud rivers to Gulashkird in Carmania, where Craterus rejoined him. Craterus had probably come by the Mulla pass, Candahar, and the Seistan lake, and had crossed the Lut by the ordinary route via Nazretabad. How Leonnatus got back is unknown.

Meanwhile Nearchus had left Kurachi. At Cocala he met Leonnatus, obtained provisions from the depot, and put all shirkers ashore and got fresh men. Thenceforth the log of the fleet resolves itself into the daily search for food and water along the inhospitable coast. Often they only got fish-meal and wild dates; sometimes they ran clean out, and Nearchus could not let the men ashore for fear of desertion. But they had some adventures. They found an enchanted mermaiden's island (Astola); they were alarmed by a school of whales, whom they charged in battle-order to the sound of the trumpet, giving thanks when the frightened monsters dived; and they discovered the Fish-eaters, the first savages any Greek had seen—a hairy stone-age people with wooden spears, who caught fish in the shallows with palm-bark nets and ate them raw or dried them in the sun and ground them into meal, wore fish-skins, and if well-to-do lived in huts built of the bones of stranded whales. At last the fleet sighted Ras Mussendam in Arabia, passed up the straits of Ormuz, and after an 80 days voyage anchored in the Amanis river; they had lost only four ships. Nearchus landed, and after various adventures found Alexander, who had been terribly anxious about the fleet, for he knew what his failure to establish depots might mean. The reunited army and fleet forgot their hardships in a round of feasting and athletic sports, a necessary holiday which legend perverted into a story of Alexander, dressed as the god Dionysus, reeling through Carmania at the head of a drunken rout. An Alexandria was founded at Gulashkird; then both army and fleet proceeded to Susa, which was reached in spring 324.

It was time that Alexander returned; his Empire could not function by itself, and he found it in great confusion. Some satraps had enrolled mercenaries and acted as independent rulers; some of the Persian satraps had ill-used and murdered their subjects. Pretenders had appeared in Media and Carmania. The tomb of Cyrus and several temples had been plundered, and two-thirds of the enormous royal stud of horses in Nisaea stolen; three of the generals in Media had joined in the campaign of wrong-doing. Cleomenes in Egypt had been guilty of many abuses; Harpalus had acted as though king, and had already fled to Greece; he was subsequently killed by one of his lieutenants. Alexander was determined not to permit oppression of subjects, and he struck very hard. He put to death the Persian satraps of Persis, Susiana, Carmania, and Media Paraetacene, and also the three generals in Media, including Cleander and Sitalces, who had killed Parmenion; Sitalces was a Thracian chieftain, but Cleander was a Macedonian aristocrat, Coenus' brother. Craterus had already captured the Carmanian pretender; Atropates now brought in the Median, who was executed. Aristobulus was commissioned to restore Cyrus' tomb; and all satraps were ordered to disband mercenaries enlisted for their private service. The vacant satrapies were perforce given to Macedonians. Tlepolemus received Carmania, and Sibyrtius three satrapies, Arachosia, Gedrosia and the Oreitae; the Indian satrapy of Philippus, who had been murdered, was entrusted provisionally to Eudamus and Taxiles. The most important matter was to quiet the minds of the Persians; Peucestas was made a Bodyguard and appointed satrap of Persis and Susiana. Peucestas was ready to carry out Alexander's ideas as he understood them; he adopted Persian dress, learnt Persian, and became extremely popular with his people. One trouble, a revolt of Greek mercenaries in Bactria, was not really overcome; Amyntas was replaced by another Philippus, but the discontent simmered till Alexander died.

At Susa a strange incident happened. Alexander was supposed, while in India, to have been interested in some ascetics, living in meditation in the forest, who told him that his conquests meant nothing at all, and that he owned precisely what they owned, as much ground as you could stand on. One of them, Calanus, accompanied the army, and is said to have taught Lysimachus; but, if his teaching was to master yourself and not others, Lysimachus did not profit by it. At Susa Calanus fell ill, and told Alexander that he desired to live no longer. Alexander demurred; but Calanus had his way, a pyre was built, and the Indian burnt himself alive in the presence of the army, while the trumpets sounded and the elephants gave the royal salute. He was said to have prophesied Alexander's death; he took farewell of the generals but not of Alexander, only saying to him 'We shall meet again at Babylon.'

At Susa too a great feast was held to celebrate the conquest of the Persian empire, at which Alexander and

80 of his officers married girls of the Iranian aristocracy, he and Hephaestion wedding Darius' daughters Barsine and Drypetis. It was an attempt to promote the fusion of Europe and Asia by intermarriage. Little came of it, for many of the bridegrooms were soon to die, and many others repudiated their Asiatic wives after Alexander's death; Seleucus, who married Spitamenes' daughter Apama, probably an Achaemenid on her mother's side, was an honourable and politic exception. At the same time 10,000 of the troops married their native concubines. Alexander undertook to pay the army's debts, and invited all debtors to inscribe their names. It is significant of the growing tension between him and his men that they at once suspected that this was merely a trick to discover those who had exceeded their pay; he thereon paid all comers in cash without asking names. But the tension grew from another cause. The governors of the new cities came bringing for enrolment in the army the 30,000 native youths who had received Macedonian training; this inflamed the discontent already aroused among the Macedonians by several of Alexander's acts, the enrolment of Asiatic cavalry in the hipparchies and of Persian nobles in the *agēma*, and the Persian dress worn by himself and Peucestas. Alexander, they felt, was no longer their own king, but an Asiatic ruler.

It was now that Alexander issued his decree to the Greek cities of the League of Corinth [1] ordering them to receive back their exiles and their families, except the Thebans, a decree read out at the Olympic games (September 324) to 20,000 exiles who had assembled to hear it and who naturally received it with enthusiasm. His object was twofold.

1 See App. 22, III, p. 370, n. 1. It did not affect the Greek cities of Asia Minor.

He wished to remove the danger to security involved in this floating mass of homeless men, ready to serve anyone as mercenaries; in this sense the decree was the logical outcome of his order to his satraps to disband their private troops. He also entertained the impossible idea of putting an end to Greek faction-fights, with their accompaniments of banishment and confiscation, and securing unity in Greece, even at his own expense; for, just as in the Greek cities of Asia he had for this purpose restrained his friends the democrats, so he now proposed to recall, among others, his enemies, the democrats exiled through Antipater's measures. Antipater had been interfering with the form of government, and the Greek democracies hated him. The story that, after Gaugamela, Alexander had ordered him to abolish his tyrants may not be true; but certainly a necessary condition of unity in Greece was his supersession. The attempt, however, to show that there was bad feeling between Alexander and Antipater is only later propaganda; there was in fact complete mutual loyalty, though doubtless Antipater wearied Alexander with his complaints, however well-founded, about Olympias; Alexander said Antipater could never understand that one tear of Olympias' would outweigh all his despatches. But a new policy required a new man; and Alexander arranged that Craterus and Antipater should change places.

The recall of the exiles was in itself a wise and statesman-like measure. But it was also a breach of the Covenant of the League of Corinth, which forbade interference with the internal affairs of the constituent states. Of course Alexander's mere existence was a continuing breach of the Covenant, for in some cities his name was keeping a minority in power; the dead pressure on the League due to its President being also the autocrat of Asia was severe. That he could not help. But for his active breach of the Covenant he contemplated the strange remedy already foreshadowed by his attempt at Bactra to introduce prostration. The Covenant bound Alexander of Macedon; it would not bind Alexander the god; the way therefore to exercise authority in the cities was to become a god. The exiles decree was therefore accompanied, or possibly even preceded, by a request to the cities of the League for his deification.[1] Most of the cities of the League, even Sparta, made no difficulty about this, and proceeded to deify him. Athens, however, irreconcilably opposed to the exiles decree (for she had expelled the Samians and colonised Samos, and the decree meant that she would have to give the Samians back their island), at first opposed Alexander's deification also, and only fell into line when she found that he was in earnest and that the risk in opposing him was serious; she then too made him a god,[2] hoping that this might placate him in the matter of Samos. By deifying Alexander, the cities, in form, condoned his breach of the Covenant; but subsequent events seem to show that in many cases their action, like that of Athens, was an unwilling one, due to fear. If we look at facts, therefore, and not forms, we must conclude that Alexander was not justified in what he did; it was simply the old trouble of the world, doing wrong for a good end. There is nothing to show that he had any intention of doing away with Greek freedom; Craterus' instructions[3] to supervise the freedom of the Hellenes, that is, to take Antipater's place

---

1 For what follows see App. 22, III.
2 The hard-worked story that he became a particular god, Dionysus, has long been exploded, see App. 22, III, p. 370, n. 2.   3 Arr. VII, 12, 4.

as deputy Hegemon of the League, show that the exiles decree was treated as an exceptional measure and that the League was to continue as before. But Alexander had taken the first step on the road of interference in the internal affairs of the cities; and he had sworn not to interfere. That the interference was badly needed does not mend the matter. What it might have led him to, had he lived, cannot be said; we know to what it led some of his Successors, but they were not Alexander.

Alexander's request for deification was seemingly brought before the League States by his partisans in the several cities, but certainly the initiative came from him and not from the Greeks; Hypereides' evidence seems conclusive,[1] and in any case Athens (for instance), irreconcilably opposed to the exiles decree, would not of her own motion have conferred on Alexander the means whereby he could carry that decree into effect without a formal breach of the Covenant. But the fact that the initiative came from Alexander has no real bearing on his character, for his deification had no religious import. To educated Greeks the old State religions were spiritually dead, and Alexander's deification was a product, not of religious feeling, but of disbelief; while to Alexander himself it was merely a political measure adopted for a limited political purpose, to give him, juridically, a foothold in autonomous Greek cities.[2] Greek cities are commonly said to have deified living men before, though there is serious doubt about this; in any case, no one now objected except his political

1 Hypereides *Against Demosthenes* fr. VIII, col. 31 is evidence that the request came from Alexander, though, in the circumstances of the speech, it is not necessarily evidence for what Demosthenes said.
2 App. 22, III, pp. 370 sq.

opponents, or a few old-fashioned people like Antipater, who really thought it impious.[1] The Macedonians themselves were not affected, one way or another; and they were ready enough, at Eumenes' suggestion, to worship Alexander once he was dead.

It was soon afterwards, at Opis, that the discontent in the army came to a head. Alexander was not trying to oust the Macedonians from their ancestral partnership with him, but they thought he was; he only wished to take it up into something larger, but they distrusted the changes entailed by a new world, and especially his Persian policy. The occasion was his proposal to send home with Craterus any veterans past service. The Macedonians took this to mean that he intended to transfer the seat of power from Macedonia to Asia, and the whole army except his Guard, the *agēma* of the hypaspists, broke into open mutiny; all demanded to go home, and told him to go and campaign with his father Ammon. Alexander's temper rose; after ordering his Guard to arrest the ringleaders, he passionately harangued the troops,[2] and ended by dismissing the whole army from his service. 'And now, as you all want to go, go, every one of you, and tell them at home that you deserted your king who had led you from victory to victory across the world, and left him to the care of the strangers he had conquered; and no doubt your words will win you the praises of men and the blessing of heaven. Go.' Then, after shutting himself up for two days, he called the Persian leaders to him and began to form a Persian army, whose formations were to bear the old Macedonian

1 Suidas, Ἀντίπατρος· ἀσεβὲς τοῦτο κρίνας.
2 On the genuineness of the essential parts of this speech, notably the conclusion, see App. 15.

names.¹ This broke down the Macedonians; they gathered before his quarters, crying that they would not go away till he had pity on them. He came out and stood before them, with tears running down his face; one began to say 'You have made Persians your kinsmen', and he broke in 'But I make you all my kinsmen.' The army burst into wild cheers; those who would kissed him; the reconciliation was complete. Those veterans who desired (10,000) were then sent home with large presents under Craterus' leadership.

But before they went, Alexander's reconciliation with the army had been followed by a greater reconciliation.² He made a vast banquet—traditionally there were 9,000 guests—to celebrate the conclusion of peace; at his own table there sat Macedonians and Persians, the two protagonists in the great war, together with representatives of every race in his Empire and also Greeks, who were part of his world though not under his rule. The feast ended, all at his table drew wine for the libation from a huge silver crater which had once belonged to Darius, the crater which Eratosthenes or his informant was to figure as a loving-cup of the nations, and the whole 9,000 made libation together at the sound of a trumpet, as was Macedonian custom, the libation being led by Greek seers and Iranian Magi. The libation led up to, and was followed by, Alexander's prayer, in which the ceremony culminated. A few words of summary, and a brief allusion, are all that have reached us; but he prayed for peace, and that Macedonians and Persians and all the peoples of his Empire might be alike partners in the commonwealth (i.e. not merely subjects), and that the peoples of the world he knew might live to-

---

1 There is nothing to show that such an army was ever formed.
2 This paragraph is a brief summary of App. 25, VI, to which I refer.

gether in harmony and in unity of heart and mind—that *Homonoia* which for centuries the world was to long for but never to reach. He had previously said that all men were sons of one Father, and his prayer was the expression of his recorded belief that he had a mission from God to be the Reconciler of the World. Though none present could foresee it, that prayer was to be the crown of his career; he did not live to try to carry it out.

That autumn at Ecbatana his friend Hephaestion died, a severe blow to the king. Hephaestion was hardly popular; he had feuds with Craterus, Eumenes, and Olympias; but Alexander clung to him as his second self, though the reason is nowhere given. He had revived for him the Persian office of chiliarch (vizier), which to Asiatics made him the second man in the empire, and had, after returning from India, collected what remained of the original Companions into one hipparchy, and given him the command.[1] He now ordered that a royal pyre should be built in Babylon and Hephaestion be honoured as a hero. Hephaestion's command was not filled up; his hipparchy was to bear his name for ever. No new chiliarch was appointed, but probably Perdiccas did the duties of the office. Alexander relieved his sorrow by a successful winter campaign in the hills of Luristan against the Cossaeans, who perhaps had demanded their customary blackmail for passage through their land. In the spring of 323 he returned to Babylon, which was destined for his capital; there envoys came to him from the Libyans and from three peoples of Italy—the Bruttians and Lucanians, who feared vengeance for the death of Alexander of Epirus, his brother-in-law, and the Etruscans, who desired freedom of the seas for

1 App. I, IV, p. 166.

their piracies.[1] Much later, a story was invented that embassies came to him from all over the known world, desiring him to settle their differences, so that he appeared to be lord of the whole earth and sea.[2]

He now again attacked the secret of the ocean. He sent Heracleides to explore the Hyrcanian sea, and ascertain whether Aristotle had been right in calling this great expanse of salt water a lake,[3] or whether the old theory that it was a gulf of Ocean might not be true after all; the project was abandoned on his death. He himself turned his attention to the Persian Gulf. He took steps to ensure better communication between Babylonia and the sea by removing the Persian obstacles to free navigation of the Tigris and founding an Alexandria on the Gulf at 'the mouth of that river, which, refounded later as Charax-Mesene, became an important trade centre; and he began to build a vast harbour-basin for merchantmen at Babylon. He also planned to colonise the eastern coast of the Gulf, along which Nearchus had sailed, and sent 500 talents to Sidon to be coined for the hire or purchase of sailors and colonists. This would help to establish the already explored sea-route between India and Babylon; but he meant to complete the sea-route from India to Egypt by exploring the section between Babylon and Egypt and circumnavigating Arabia, possibly as a preliminary to still more extensive maritime exploration in the future. He therefore planned an expedition along the Arabian coast, and for this purpose had a few larger warships, including quinqueremes,

1 Arr. VII, 15, 4, from the *Journal* (in which all embassies would be recorded) through Ptolemy. These four embassies are certain.
2 App. 23. On the fictitious Roman embassy see § C, pp. 21–5.
3 See § B, pp. 6 sq.

built in sections in Phoenicia, carried to Thapsacus, and
floated down the Euphrates. It was to be primarily a naval
expedition and voyage of exploration,[1] though supported
by troops, and the *Journal* shows that he himself was going
with the fleet; it was reported that he did not mean to
make Arabia a province under a satrap.[2] He knew little
of Arabia except the districts bordering on Babylonia and
Syria, once subject (rather nominally) to Persia; Nearchus
had sighted Ras Mussendam, but it might have been an
island. Being ignorant of its size, he attempted a preliminary circumnavigation from both sides; he sent a ship
south from the gulf of Suez under Anaxicrates which
reached the incense-land of Yemen and heard of the
Hadramaut,[3] and three triakontors down the Persian Gulf.
One discovered the island of Bahrein; Hieron of Soli,
whose orders were to sail round to Suez, followed the
Arabian coast down to Ras Mussendam, and wisely reported that Arabia must be nearly as big as India.

While the fleet was preparing, Alexander sailed down the
Euphrates to study the Babylonian canal-system, and
especially the Pallakopas cut, which carried off the flood
water of the river; it was not working well, and he devised
a better method for keeping the Euphrates at the proper
level for irrigation; he also founded a city on the Chaldean
side of the lower Euphrates as an outpost towards Arabia.
The story was told that on the voyage his diadem blew off
and lodged on a rush; a sailor swam out for it, and to keep
it dry placed it on his head; later a legend grew up that the

1 As regards the land force the *Journal* called it a πορεία, Arr. VII, 25, 2, and
  as regards the fleet a πλοῦς, Arr. ibid. 2 to 5, Plut. *Alex.* LXXVI; it is nowhere
  called a στρατεία.
2 Arr. VII, 20, I.
3 Tarn, *J.E.A.* XV, 1929, p. 13.

man who for a moment had worn Alexander's diadem was
Seleucus. On his return to Babylon Alexander is said to
have remodelled the phalanx, incorporating Persian light-
armed; it is not known ever to have been used, but
something of the sort is alluded to in a late tactical manual.[1]
Antipater's eldest son Cassander now came to him, to
answer accusations against Antipater made by some
Illyrians and Thracians. Also there came many envoys
from Greece, with petitions on innumerable questions
raised by the exiles decree; they came garlanded, as though
they had been religious envoys sent to a god.

They set the stage for the final scene. For in the midst
of his preparations for the Arabian expedition Alexander
was struck down by a fever, which his constitution,
weakened by over-exertion and wounds, could not throw
off. The *Journal* relates that for some days he continued his
preparations, offering the usual sacrifices and discussing
the coming expedition with his generals and Ocean with
Nearchus, till he became too ill to move; then he was
carried into Nebuchadrezzar's palace, already past speech.
The army insisted on seeing him, and would take no denial;
in silence the veterans filed through the room where the
dying man lay, just able to raise his head in token of
recognition and farewell. That night several of the generals
inquired of some Babylonian god[2] if Alexander should be
brought into his temple; the oracle replied that it would be
best for him where he was. Two days later, at sunset, he died;
for that was best. He died on 13 June 323; he was not yet
33 years old, and had reigned twelve years and eight months.

1 Asclepiodotus 6; first century B.C.
2 Arr. VII, 26, 2, from the *Journal*. But it was Ptolemy, not the *Journal*, who
called the god Sarapis; it was part of the propaganda for that deity, which
became so lively under Ptolemy II.

CHAPTER THREE

PERSONALITY, POLICY AND AIMS

LEXANDER was fortunate in his death. His fame could hardly have increased; but it might perhaps have been diminished. For he died with the real task yet before him. He had made war as few have made it; it remained to be seen if he could make peace. He had, like Columbus, opened up a new world; it remained to be seen what he could do with it. No man since has possessed so unquestionably the strongest power upon earth; had he desired, he could have conquered either Carthage or Rome, though he could have done nothing with them had he conquered them; he could do nothing even with the Punjab. But there is no reason to suppose that he had formed any design of world-conquest. In fact, he had not yet completed the conquest of the one-time Persian empire; a great block of territory stretching from Heraclea to the Caspian—Paphlagonia, Cappadocia, Pontus, Armenia, the Cadusii of Gilan—had become independent, and the dangerous bottleneck on his communications across Asia Minor still existed, to be removed by Perdiccas as soon as he was dead. His desire to reach the (supposed) eastern Ocean was not a desire to round off his Empire on all sides with Ocean;[1] had it been, he would not have turned at the Jaxartes, where (with Aristotle) he thought Ocean quite close, and the expeditions he was planning when he died to explore the Caspian and the coast of South Arabia would have been schemes of conquest, not of exploration. What

1 In effect the desire attributed to Pompey, Plut. *Pomp.* XXXVIII.

ought to be conclusive is that, after his hard-won conquest of the eastern Punjab, he made no attempt to hold that country but just handed it over to Porus as an independent monarch; that is not how would-be world-conquerors act. He never even, like the Achaemenids, called himself king of kings. That he aimed at world-dominion, as so many have believed,[1] is only an invention of a later day, worked up in modern times. It rested originally on two things. One was the supposed promise of world-rule made to him by Ammon, long since shown to be a mere derivation from the Amon-ritual, in which Amon promised the dominion of the earth to every new Pharaoh, however insignificant, at his coronation; that has now been dropped. The other is a late and unauthentic collection of plans which has passed as his Memoirs (or Memoranda) and which attributes to him a scheme for the conquest of the countries round the Mediterranean,[2] a scheme which late versions of the Romance afterwards made him carry into effect. It could doubtless be suggested that if he desired to unite all peoples in *Homonoia* he must have desired to conquer them first; but that would be mere speculation, and history has no right to attribute any such ideas to Alexander. What he would have aimed at, had he lived, we do not know; we can only try to see what he was and what he did.

His personality was adequate to great tasks. Aristotle had presumably taught him that man's highest good lay in right activity of the soul; he had modified this for himself into strenuous energy of soul and body both. He had crowded as much into his short life as he could; when he

1 It has been an article of faith with modern German scholars. An older generation in that country thought differently.
2 See App. 24, *Alexander's supposed Plans.*

died, his body was half worn out. But his vitality of mind was unimpaired; and his mind could generally make his body do what it chose. For, as Plutarch says,[1] he thought it more kingly to conquer himself than others; and he gives a strangely vivid impression of one whose body was his servant. This is the key to his attitude toward women;[2] apart from his mother, he apparently never cared for any woman; he apparently never had a mistress, and his two marriages were mere affairs of policy. When he called his beautiful Persian captives 'painful to the eyes', what he meant is, in Plutarch's narrative, fairly obvious: women were merely incitements to the rebellion of the body. The phenomenon has since become well known; but it made Alexander, to his contemporaries, seem either more, or less, than a man. It meant a will of iron; but even his will was inadequate for one end, the control of his temper. The son of Olympias was bound to be shaken by devastating gusts of passion; but though this showed in impatience, in irritability, in decisions repented of later, only once, apparently, did he absolutely lose control; then his wrath swept to its goal in total disregard of every other consideration, human or divine. The murder of Cleitus gives a fearful glimpse of the wild beast in him that he had to keep chained; his anguish after the deed was perhaps not only for his friend but for himself. It gives too a glimpse of the power of will that could usually keep such a beast chained. But if his temperament led him sometimes to grievous acts of injustice, it led him also to acts of justice far in advance

1 Plut. *Alex.* XXI.
2 For all that follows see App. 18. For 'Barsine', see App. 20. My reasons for using much of Plut. *Alex.* XXI, XXII, are given in App. 16, p. 298; see also App. 18, p. 322, n. 5, and Addenda to p. 298.

of his time, like his unheard-of step of ordering Parmenion to put two Macedonians on trial for rape and kill them like animals if convicted. His clemency is often mentioned, and he is perhaps the only character in Greek public life who is ever recorded to have felt pity.[1] What his force of character was like can be best seen, not in his driving power, great as it was, but in his relations with his generals. Here was an assembly of kings, with passions, ambitions, abilities beyond those of most men; and, while he lived, all we see is that Perdiccas and Ptolemy were good brigade-leaders, Antigonus an obedient satrap, Lysimachus and Peithon little-noticed members of the Staff; even on the masterful Cassander he so imposed himself during their brief acquaintance that a story grew up that he had been unable to pass Alexander's statue at Delphi without shivering.[2]

These are some of the things that seem to stand out most clearly in his picture. But there was another side, which cannot be overlooked; a romanticism which was kindled by the exploits of Achilles and Heracles, Semiramis and Cyrus, and burst into flame under the glamour of the East; something too of the mystic which set him apart from others as the man whom Ammon had counselled, and who possibly felt himself an instrument of the gods. From this side of him, obscurely as we see it, sprang what was probably the most important thing about him: he was a great dreamer. To be mystical and intensely practical, to dream greatly and to do greatly, is not given to many men; it is this combination which gives Alexander his place apart in

1 See § F, p. 65.
2 Plut. *Alex.* LXXIV. The rest of LXXIV, however, is certainly untrue; for part of it, see App. 16, p. 299.

history. There were of course terrible crimes in his record—the destruction of Thebes, the murder of Parmenion, the Massaga massacre—the sins of a young and imperious man who meant to rule because he could. None need palliate them; perhaps those only who have known the temptations of power can judge.

That he was a great general is certain; Napoleon's verdict suffices. The few who have doubted have either believed the fantastic legend which makes the Persian armies huge useless mobs, or have suggested that his success was due to Parmenion and the Staff. Alexander started of course with the advantage of Philip's army; but Parmenion's death made no apparent difference, while his Staff in Turkestan and India were men he had trained himself. Probably he was not tested to the full, unless at Tyre and on the Jhelum; but that he would have been equal to almost any test is shown by the manner in which he met every opponent with different but appropriate tactics; he handled the unknown foe—Saca nomads, Indian hill-tribes, Porus' elephants—with the same certainty as Greek hoplites or Persian cavalry. If he charged himself, so did every general before Hannibal; the use of reserves was practically unknown, and the moral effect all-important. He was a master in the combination of various arms; he taught the world the advantages of campaigning in winter, the value of pressing pursuit to the utmost,[1] and the principle of 'march divided, fight united'. He marched usually in two divisions, one conducting the impedimenta and his own travelling light; his speed of movement was extraordinary. It is said that one element of his success consisted

1 This, however, he may have learnt from Philip: U. Wilcken, *S.B. Berlin*, XVIII, 1929, p. 298 [10], n. 6.

in 'never putting anything off'.[1] He understood absolutely how to keep his men's affection; and though their moral broke at the Beas, he had maintained it intact during eight strenuous years. He discovered the value of amusements in this respect, and held athletic and musical contests at every important halting-place. The enormous distances traversed in unknown country (though he had the benefit of the Persian road system) imply a very high degree of organising ability; in ten years he had only two serious breakdowns, his intelligence before Issus and his commissariat in Gedrosia, the latter partly due to the bad luck of Apollophanes' death. The truth is, that his success was too complete. Perfect success invariably looks easy; but had a lesser man attempted what he achieved, and failed, we should have heard enough of the hopeless military difficulties of the undertaking. Did Crassus or Antony find the invasion of Persia easy?

Whether he was a great statesman is a more difficult question. Our information is inadequate, and his work was only beginning when death cut it short; no formal answer is possible. Something was wanted to divert his energy whole-heartedly from war and exploration to administration. The chaos in his Empire when he returned from India should have called out his powers in this direction; but he was preoccupied with the completion of the sea-route from India to Egypt, and he merely hanged some satraps and appointed others. Unless in the Punjab, he had nowhere gone beyond the boundaries of Darius I; and he naturally retained the Persian system of great satrapies. But it does not follow that that system would have been his last word. He abolished it in Egypt, and substituted an arrangement

[1] F, § p. 75, n. 4.

more enlightened than that which the Ptolemies subsequently adopted; and even in Iran it may have been largely provisional. For the Alexandrias were not meant to be satrapal seats[1]—there were no less than four in the old Bactrian satrapy and none in Persis, Parthia, and perhaps Media; and the separation of the Indian districts west of the Indus, and the formation of little satrapies like Media Paraetacene and the Oreitae, may suggest that he would ultimately have aimed at achieving greater centralisation by breaking up the old satrapies into smaller and more manageable units, anticipating the inevitable development which began when the Seleucids subdivided the old satrapies into eparchies and ended when the Graeco-Bactrians, Parthians, and all the smaller Seleucid Succession states turned the Seleucid eparchies into satrapies. In any event he greatly restricted the satraps' powers; they lost the right to collect taxes and (except at Babylon) to strike coins, while the chief fortresses were held by governors directly responsible to himself. Any subject who was wronged could, as in Macedonia, appeal to Alexander direct. For anything but satrapal government in some form Asia was not ripe; whether it would ripen must depend on the measures adopted to that end, and time.

Meanwhile the most important of the peoples in his world were not in his Empire at all, and his relations with the Greeks had fallen into two compartments, omitting those cities on the Black Sea and west of the Adriatic with which he had no relations at all. It was a statesmanlike policy to treat the old Greek cities of Asia as his free allies; but in Greece itself he had inherited Philip's policy, and his rights and duties in regard to the cities were formulated

1 App. 8, 1, p. 247.

and limited by the Covenant of the League of Corinth, of which he was Hegemon. That League was an attempt to unite a country disunited by nature and traditional sentiment. It had its points—for example, it gave the small cities proportionate rights over against the large ones, and some of them regarded it as a charter of liberty; but on the whole the Greeks had no desire to make it work. Few desired unification, some regretted the loss of a separate foreign policy, and many regarded the League merely as an instrument of foreign control: the delegates met under the shadow of the Macedonian garrison on Acrocorinthus. Had Alexander lived, he would have had to do something about the difference in his relations with the Greek world on the two sides of the Aegean; but we neither know what he thought nor see what he could have done.

It will be convenient to consider Alexander's measures for his Empire generally under four heads: finance, the new cities, fusion, and the general question of co-ordination.

Alexander's financial superintendents were a new and important thing, and the system survived his death. Probably they and their district subordinates were meant to form a comprehensive Civil Service, with Harpalus at its head, which would link up king and peasant. Unfortunately we do not know in what relation they stood to the satraps, or how the latter obtained the necessary funds for administering their satrapies. Harpalus' position, however, was superior to that of any satrap; he could give the satraps orders,[1] and this explains how he tried to lord it as king during Alexander's absence, an extraordinary

---

1 His powers were presumably not less than those of his successor Antimenes, who did give such orders: Ps. Arist. *Oec.* II, 34, 38.

phenomenon in a civilian without military powers. His successor Antimenes introduced the first known scheme of insurance.[1] The system should have benefited the peasantry by preventing indiscriminate exactions; and we hear of no complaint that taxes were too high. But during Alexander's absence it did not work well. Harpalus, himself corrupt, was not the man to repress exactions; the satraps, by ways familiar in Asia, got money enough to raise private armies; and a surviving document[2] gives rather a lurid account of the sins of some of the financial officials. It may be liberally discounted, for it represents an attempt by some Peripatetic to belittle Alexander's administration; but doubtless things did not go well while he was in India, and the guilt of the worst offender, the Greek Cleomenes in Egypt, is corroborated from better sources.[3] It may be that his famous corner in grain did not hurt the Egyptian cultivator; but his prohibition of any export but his own must have half ruined the Egyptian merchants, the prices at which he sold were a method of plundering Greek cities, and the money he exacted from the temples and other acts of oppression must have caused grievous discontent. He amassed 8,000 talents by his misdeeds, a fantastic sum at a time when the richest man in Greece was perhaps worth 160 talents;[4] even Harpalus, with Alexander's treasure at command, only managed to steal 5,000 talents. Alexander, far away at Susa with his hands very full, may not, before he died, have realised, or even known, what was happening in Egypt. In any case, the story that he pardoned Cleomenes and licensed him to sin as he pleased for the future comes from

1 Ps. Arist. *Oec.* II, 34. 2 Ibid. II, 31; 33–4; 38–9.
3 Arr. VII, 23, 6; Dem. LVI, 7.
4 Diphilus: Plut. *Mor.* 843 D (doubtfully).

a forged letter, and is untrue;[1] he had just put a highly placed Macedonian aristocrat, Cleander, to death for oppression of subjects, and could not after that have pardoned a Greek financier for the same offence.

Of great importance was the coinage. The problem was to reconcile the decimal coinage of Persia (1 gold daric = 20 silver sigloi) with the duodecimal of Philip II (1 gold stater, Attic standard = 24 silver drachmae, Phoenician standard). Alexander did it by reverting to a silver monometallism and adopting the Attic standard, thus making the stater = 20 silver drachmae, which, though lighter than sigloi, were accepted in Asia. He thus refrained from competing with Athens' coinage, and practically made her a trade partner; but he demonetised the Persian gold, for as the hoarded treasures of Darius began to circulate gold fell below Philip's basic ratio, and the daric became bullion. The uniform coinage powerfully promoted trade, but whether the credit for the adoption of the Attic standard as an auxiliary in conquering Asia belongs to Alexander may be doubted; for as he adopted the new standard the moment Philip died, it may be that Philip had already decided on the change. Only two countries disliked the new coinage— conservative India, and the Balkans, which Alexander had neglected. He continued to use nearly all the existing Persian mints, except Tyre and Gaza. But his principal mint was at Amphipolis, with Babylon second in importance; next came the Phoenician group (Sidon, Byblus, Ake, Damascus), the Cilician (Tarsus and Alexandria by Issus, with the independent Cyprian mints), and Alexandria by Egypt; there were many others, including Pella the

1 On Alexander's alleged letter to Cleomenes, Arr. VII, 23, 6, see App. 16, pp. 303–6.

capital. His mints must have been controlled by royal officials, but to whom these were responsible is unknown; Tarsus, however, became the financial centre for Asia Minor and the eastern Mediterranean, and Harpalus had his seat there as well as at Babylon. But Alexander showed his wisdom by not forcing the new coinage wholesale on the great trading centres, Phoenicia, Cilicia, and Babylon; there he still permitted the old coinage to be struck also, as a temporary measure.[1]

These were two great financial reforms. But the treasury still remained identical with the king's privy purse; and when Alexander's natural generosity and his enormous expenditure are considered, one wonders whether, had he lived, he would have been able to balance his accounts.[2] He gave 2,000 talents to the Thessalians and allies, and a talent each to the 10,000 discharged Macedonian veterans; 20,000 talents were used to pay the army's debts, and 15,000 for gold crowns for the generals; at the marriages at Susa he gave dowries to 80 noble Persian girls and 10,000 women of the people; he allocated 10,000 talents to Hephaestion's pyre, and there were presents for Indian princes, artistes, and learned men, including 800 talents for Aristotle's researches.[3] He had too an amazing programme of works in hand when he died; it included some unfinished cities;

---

1 For the mints see the works of Mr E. T. Newell given in *C.A.H.* VI, pp. 593 sq., A 2.

2 There is a large element of guesswork in these accounts. They have been considered in detail by A. Andréadès, Ἱστορία τῆς Ἑλληνικῆς δημοσίας οἰκονομίας II, part I: ἡ δημοσία οἰκονομία τοῦ μεγάλου Ἀλεξάνδρου, 1930, pp. 47–74. He decided that they could not possibly have balanced in 324/3 and 323/2; after that, Alexander would have raised enough income (p. 74) by increasing taxation and overhauling sources of revenue.

3 Athen. IX, 398 E; see, however, Gercke, 'Aristoteles' col. 1018, in PW.— Some of the foregoing monetary figures may be exaggerated.

two temples at Sardis and Ilium;[1] the new docks and harbours at Patala and Babylon; improved harbour-works at Clazomenae and Erythrae;[2] the rebuilding of E-sagila, destroyed by Xerxes, where the arduous work of merely clearing the site of ruins was still going on in 310;[3] the restoration and amelioration of the Babylonian canal system; the draining of Lake Copais.[4] Except Hephaestion's pyre, most of this expenditure was justifiable in itself. The army was entitled to share Darius' gold; the dowries were part of a great policy; the Indian princes gave as much as they received; most of the works except the temples would have been remunerative, and E-sagila was provided for by special local taxation. But if we add the expenses of the war,[5] and the money squandered and stolen by Harpalus, the story might be correct that, in spite of Alexander's large revenue, probably some 15,000 talents a year,[6] out of all the treasure he had secured only 50,000 talents remained at his death.[7]

We come to the new cities. Isocrates had advised Philip to build cities in Asia and to settle the homeless mercenaries in them;[8] and Alexander was one of the greatest city-

---

1 Sardis, Arr. I, 17, 5; Ilium, Strab. XIII, 1, 26 (593).   2 Pliny V, 116, 117.
3 S. Smith, *Babylonian Historical Texts*, no. 5, A chronicle concerning the Diadochi.   4 Strab. IX, 2, 18 (407); Steph. 'Aθῆναι.
5 Beloch, *Gr. Gesch.*² IV, 1, 42 put these at 7,000 talents a year at the least, Andréadès, op cit. p. 71, at 10,000, both figures relating to Alexander's last years. But the number of men he was paying, garrisons included, is pure guesswork, and varied considerably.
6 Both Beloch (ibid. p. 43) and Andréadès (op. cit. p. 59) have put his revenue at not under 15,000 talents a year, which is reasonable, since Antigonus' income in 315, off a much smaller territory, was 11,000 talents, Diod. XIX, 56, 5 (from Hieronymus).
7 Just. XIII, 1, 9; worth little, as the same sentence makes his income 30,000 talents a year.
8 Isoc. *Phil.* 106.

builders of all time.[1] He is said to have founded over
70, but that is a great exaggeration; 16 Alexandrias are
certain, another (Alexandretta) practically certain, and there
are one or two more perhaps just possible, together with
an unknown number of military colonies.[2] All the cities
were officially named Alexandria, though in many cases
only the nicknames of popular usage have come down to
us;[3] and all those certain, except Alexandria by Egypt and
Alexandretta, were east of the Tigris. Nearly all were new
foundations, though some might replace a native village;
only one, Bactra, seems to have been a native town
hellenised, and there is no other certain case of one being
founded at the seat of a Persian satrap. The swollen figure
of tradition was probably helped out by the inclusion of
cities which he planned or promised and others built, like
Smyrna and Alexandria Troas; of cities which other
builders attributed to him or which attributed themselves;
of military colonies, which so often grew into cities; and
of cities given him by romance, like Samarcand and Sian-
fu. The Seleucid kings continued his building policy on a
comprehensive scale; but all his Successors caught something of his inspiration and did some building, even his
enemy Cassander, who founded Salonica. Alexander in
fact initiated what became a vast scheme of colonisation in
Asia, differing from the older Greek colonisation in that it
was deliberately planned, that many cities were not on the
sea, and that the settlers were not drawn from single cities
but were mixed. The typical Alexandria was settled with

1 On Alexander's foundations see App. 8.
2 On the military colony see Tarn, *Bactria and India*, pp. 6–11 and references.
  There may have been more than one type.
3 For the nomenclature see Tarn, op. cit. pp. 12–16.

Greek mercenaries, traders, natives, and a few Macedonians. But this was only to start with. For the Greek mercenaries had native wives, and were not the best medium for the spread of Greek culture; Alexander probably meant to send out further settlers, and above all European women, to prevent the risk of the towns becoming purely Asiatic, as some of the original Greek colonies in Aeolis had done. That Asia was not more hellenised than it was arose simply from there not being enough Greeks in the world. They had to be collected into comparatively few towns; they never spread over the country. It has been suggested that it would have been better for Greek civilisation had Alexander confined his conquests to Asia Minor, which could have been governed from Europe, and attempted a more intensive hellenisation. In this event, however, Greeks would not have secured a share in the great trade routes; they could not do both.

Simple hellenisation, moreover, was not his object; and he did not, like Eumenes and possibly Antigonus, propose to oust any Iranian landowners. As his marriage to Roxane had guaranteed her class, and he meant the Iranian landowners and the new towns to co-exist, it cannot be supposed that his ultimate aim was an Empire divided up into city states; for, as the new towns were designed to promote the fusion of Europe and Asia on a basis of Greek culture, they were probably not autonomous Greek cities but a new mixed type. Most of what we know about Alexander's towns relates to Alexandria by Egypt, and there it is impossible to distinguish what is original and what not; but the *type* was doubtless due to Alexander, for Ptolemy I's foundation Ptolemaïs was an autonomous Greek city. A provisional sketch of one of the Alexandrias under

Alexander may therefore be attempted.[1] It was founded on King's land, and would consist of a Greek corporation and probably other national corporations—Thracians, Persians, etc.—each possessing certain quasi-autonomous rights; probably also a few privileged Macedonians, and some local natives. The Greek corporation was much the most important; they were 'the citizens', 'the Alexandrians'. The constitutive law of the city, given by Alexander, created officials of Greek type and prescribed their duties; these must have acted for the whole city, e.g. the astynomi would look after *all* the streets, whatever the nationality of the householders. It seems probable that there was neither Council[2] nor Assembly; but there were autonomous Greek law-courts which, independently of the king, administered a body of private law formed by royal rescripts and the 'city law', this last a code based on, or taken bodily from, that of some leading Greek city. This code may have been settled by a commission (nomographi) appointed at Alexander's instance; but doubtless in the more remote foundations he merely ordered that some well-known code should be adopted. The important thing is that *all* the inhabitants were in practice subject, not only to the king's rescripts, largely based on Greek legal conceptions, but probably also to the 'city law',[3] which was in principle the personal law of the Greek 'citizens'. Thus there might develop a territorial law embracing the whole city; and possibly Alexander deliberately meant to use Greek law,

1 What follows is founded on *Dikaiomata, Auszüge aus Alexandrinischen Gesetzen herausgegeben von der Graeca Halensis* (=P. Hal. 1), 1913.
2 Whether at a later time Alexandria by Egypt had a Council or not has been the subject of much discussion.
3 The Jewish community in the Egyptian Alexandria was subsequently an exception.

rather than political rights, as one means of unifying these mixed city populations. One recalls that his financial superintendents leased King's land in Asia according to Greek law (see p. 30, n. 1).

It is possible that one of the differences[1] between the Greek city and the military colony was that the city was absolute owner of its city-land while in the military colony the settler's allotments remained King's land, the king retaining the right of escheat; this right appears in the Succession Law of Doura-Europus,[2] which dated from the first days of the colony,[3] and the same document shows that the succession to all allotments was regulated by Greek law, whatever the settler's nationality. Whether evidence derived from this later settlement can be applied to Alexander's new cities may be disputable; but it would make sense, for politically his cities, unlike the old Greek cities of Asia, were subject to governors appointed by himself,[4] and possibly to his satraps; in Greek eyes they therefore approximated somewhat to the native subject towns, and it is related that the Greeks settled in the far East refused to regard this mixed system as Hellenic 'life and training'.[5] Whether Alexander intended that these towns should, after a period of probation, acquire full autonomous Greek rights cannot be said; they certainly did later.[6]

1 Tarn, *Bactria and India*, p. 31.
2 Published by B. Haussoullier, *Rev. hist. du droit français et étranger*, 1923, p. 515; other references in Tarn, op. cit. p. 7, n. 5.
3 P. Koschaker, *Zeits. Sav. Stiftung, Rom. Abt.*, XLVI, p. 297.
4 Arr. IV, 22, 4; VII, 6, 1, where σατράπαι means governors, ὕπαρχοι; on Arrian's loose use of these terms, see App. 3, p. 173, n. 1.
5 Diod. XVIII, 7, 1.
6 Specific evidence exists for Alexandria 'of the Tigris', the later Charax Spasinu, Tarn, op. cit. p. 17. It must have been the same for all; on those in India, Tarn, op. cit., passim.

Next, Alexander's policy of the fusion of races. It was a great and courageous idea, which, as he planned it, failed. He might indeed fairly have supposed that his experiment in mixed marriages would be successful, for he only applied it to Asia and it only meant marriage between different branches of the white race. Greek blood had once been mixed with Anatolian with good results in Miletus and many other cities, as with Libyan (Berber) blood in Cyrene; Herodotus and Themistocles were half-breeds, while the intermarriage of Macedonian and Iranian was to produce that great organiser Antiochus I; but, speaking broadly, the better-class Greeks and Macedonians now refused to cooperate.[1] And it is doubtful whether, even had he lived, he could have carried out his idea of a joint commonwealth; for his system of Iranian satraps had broken down before he died. Of eighteen appointed, two soon died, one retired, and two are not again heard of; but ten were either removed for incompetence or executed for murder of subjects or treason, and were replaced by Macedonians. The three who alone held office when Alexander died were doubtless good men; nevertheless Atropates certainly, and Oxyartes possibly,[2] ended by founding independent Iranian kingdoms, while from Phrataphernes' satrapy of Parthia-Hyrcania came later the main Iranian reaction. In fact, Alexander had come into conflict with the idea of nationality, which was exhibited, not merely in the national war fought by Sogdiana, but in the way in which, even during

1 The attitude of the Greeks in Asia to mixed marriages is discussed, Tarn, op. cit. pp. 34–8.
2 A. de la Fuye, *Revue Numismatique*, 1910, pp. 281 sqq. (Now very doubtful; for a more probable suggestion of what happened to the Paropamisadae, see Tarn, *J.H.S.* LIX, 1939, p. 322, reviewing E. T. Newell, *The coinage of the Eastern Seleucid mints*.)

his lifetime, independent states like Cappadocia and Armenia under Iranian rulers arose along the undefined northern limits of his empire. But of course, owing to his death, his policy never had a fair trial. The Seleucid kings indeed, half Sogdian in blood, were a direct outcome of that policy, and they did carry out parts of it; they transferred Europeans to Asia, employed, though sparingly, Asiatics in high position, and produced a marvellous mixture of east and west. But it was not done on Alexander's lines or in his spirit; the Macedonian meant to be, and was, the dominant race. What Alexander did achieve was again done through the cities, both his own and those which he inspired Seleucus to found, and it was a great enough achievement; the cities radiated Greek culture throughout Asia till ultimately the bulk of the upper classes over considerable districts became partially hellenised, and Demetrius of Bactria led Greeks for a second time beyond the Hindu Kush, to succeed for a moment where Alexander had failed and rule northern India for a few years from Pātaliputra to Kathiawar. What Alexander did succeed in ultimately giving to parts of western Asia was not political equality with Greece, but community of culture.

Lastly, we have to consider the question of the co-ordination of the Empire, together with the countries which, though not actually in his Empire, were within his sphere. That Empire was even more complicated than the British. In Egypt Alexander was an autocrat and a god. In Asia he was an autocrat, but not a god. In old Greece he was a god, but not an autocrat. In Macedonia he was neither autocrat nor god, but a quasi-constitutional king over against whom his people enjoyed certain customary rights. The Phoenician kings were subject allies; the

Cyprian kings were free allies, who coined gold, the token
of independence. Persepolis kept her native priest-kings,
from whom was to spring the Sassanian dynasty; the High
Priests still governed Judaea according to the Law; the
temple states of Asia Minor retained their strange matri-
archal and theocratic social system unchanged. To the
Iranian land-owners he was feudal superior. In Lydia and
Babylon he had voluntarily limited his autocracy by native
custom; Caria retained her native league of Zeus Chrysa-
oreus; part of Seistan was autonomous. With the peoples
of the Punjab he had no point of contact; their real organisation was the village community, and Alexander was
merely for a little while the rather nominal suzerain of
certain rajahs who happened to be ruling certain groups of
villages. His relations with the Greek world were equally
complex. Philip had incorporated some Greek cities in
Macedonia; Alexander's new cities were Greek rather than
Macedonian, and several Greek or semi-Greek cities in
Pamphylia and Cilicia were his subjects. But the old Greek
cities of Asia along the Aegean and as far north as Cyzicus
were his free allies, while many Greek cities, notably those
on the Black Sea and in Italy and Sicily, had no relations
with him at all. In Thessaly he was the elected head for life
of her League; in the Amphictyonic League a man who
owned two votes. In old Greece he was President and war-
leader of the League of Corinth, but he was also something
more than that: he was the Macedonian State,[1] far the
strongest State in the League, and he was also the god of

1 Alexander's double position in the League has been curiously misunder-
stood; modern writers have often talked about 'the Macedonian state'
in the League, and wondered at its omission in the sources. There was no
Macedonian State apart from the king till Antigonus Doson; *vis-à-vis*
other Powers, the king *was* the State.

the several cities, with the undefined powers of a god. Old Greece was not in his Empire, but neither was she entirely outside it, as many Greeks knew very well; she obeyed his orders, and his deputy Antipater still retained Philip's garrisons in Corinth, Chalcis, and the Cadmea; the technical and cultural sides of the Empire were staffed entirely by Greeks. The co-ordination of this heterogeneous mass of rights was not going to be achieved by Alexander claiming (as some believe he claimed) to be the divine ruler of the inhabited world.

Fortunately there is no reason for attributing to him any such idea. He was deified in 324 by the cities of the League of Corinth only, as a limited political measure; even in those cities he did not claim to be the only god or even the supreme god, and (Greece apart) this deification had no bearing on the co-ordination of his Empire; for he was in no sense the god of that Empire, whatever he may once have thought of being. There is no trace of any common official cult of himself in his Empire; his head does not (as it would then have done) appear on the Alexander-coinage; his successor in the Empire, Philip III, was not even a god at all, except in Egypt. That Alexander, like every Pharaoh, was divine in Egypt has no bearing on the matter; the point is, that he was not divine in Iran. Zoroastrianism knew nothing of, and had no place for, deified men; and it is noteworthy that on the coins which Agathocles of Bactria struck to exhibit his pedigree,[1] though the Greeks Diodotus and Euthydemus are gods,

---

[1] I.e. the fictitious Seleucid pedigree, which began with Alexander; on this and the coins, see Tarn, *Bactria and India*, App. 3 and pp. 201 sq. I omitted to notice, among occurrences of this pedigree, the allusion to it in the Livy-Trogus speech of Mithridates, Justin xxxviii, 7, 1.

Alexander is not. We cannot read back into the tentative
events of Alexander's life considerations which, if they
arise at all, arise from the worship of him under his successors and from the phenomena of Roman Imperialism.

Whether indeed he ever meant to try to co-ordinate his
Empire, and if so how, we do not know. It is unlikely that
he had any cut-and-dried theories on the subject; but he
had initiated various measures which, in their degree, made
for unity, and he would probably have gone on in the same
way, step by step, taking things as they arose. Trade, the
coinage, the new mixed cities, might do something; something more might be done by inter-marriage, by training
native youths in Graeco-Macedonian fashion, by giving
Persians a share in the government. Babylon was probably
selected for capital as being neutral ground between the
Graeco-Macedonian and Iranian worlds, though it is not
certain that Alexandria in Egypt was not meant to be a
joint capital. But the true unifying force was lacking; there
was no common idea, or ideal. The United States has turned
men of many countries into Americans by force of the
American idea. Britain and the Dominions are held
together by a common idea stronger than any formal bond.
There was no equivalent in Alexander's sphere; there was
no common term even between Greek and Persian. To
two of the great contributions made by Greece to the
world's progress, freedom of action (so far as it went) and
freedom of thought, Persia was a stranger; and to incorporate Persia in the Empire at all Alexander had to
diminish Greek freedom of action; his new cities were
probably not autonomous Greek foundations, and with
the Greek cities themselves he began to interfere. But if
Persia could only be incorporated by lowering Greek

political values, then politically the Empire stood condemned from the start.

Security of course it could and would have given, had
Alexander lived; and behind that shield it might have
developed those possibilities of ethical and intellectual progress which constituted Alexander's greatest gift to Asia,
and might, given time enough, have achieved complete
unity of culture and therefrom created a common idea.
But all this was hypothetical, and dependent on a single
life; and, as a fact, up to Alexander's death, the Empire was
held together solely by himself and his (mixed) army; that
is, it resembled the Empire of the Hapsburgs. And a
further source of weakness was that the ultimate care of
everything—the army, administration, law—fell upon
himself personally, entailing a stupendous amount of work;
probably only his habit of occasionally sleeping for 36 hours
kept him going; certainly towards the end he was growing
more impatient and irritable. His one attempt at comprehensive delegation turned out unhappily, owing to
Harpalus' unworthiness. Nevertheless, had he lived his full
term, and trained a son, his Empire, for all its defects
politically, might well have achieved a cohesion beyond
our belief; it needed what seemed at the time the supreme
shock of all history to break up that of the Hapsburgs, and
we have to reckon, as a moulding force, with Alexander's
astounding personality.

For when all is said, we come back at the end to his
personality; not the soldier or the statesman, but the man.
Whatever Asia did or did not get from him, she *felt* him
as she has scarcely felt any other; she knew that one of the
greatest of the earth had passed. Though his direct influence
vanished from India within a generation, and her literature

does not know him, he affected Indian history for centuries; for Chandragupta saw him and deduced the possibility of realising in actual fact the conception, handed down from Vedic times, of a comprehensive monarchy in India; hence Alexander indirectly created Asoka's empire and enabled the spread of Buddhism. Possibly his example even inspired the unification of China under the first Han dynasty. Both flanks of the Hindu Kush were once full of hill chieftains who claimed descent[1] from the man who left none to succeed him. On the Indian side they once ruled in Chitral, Gilgit, Nagir, Hunza, and elsewhere, and we ourselves have seen a Mir of Hunza who was descended from Alexander and bore a British title; it is said that at one time they intermarried only with each other, and some families on both sides of the mountains seem to have acquired the Alexander-descent by marriage; the white Kafirs of Kafiristan became, and still are, Alexander's Macedonians, and in the Middle Ages an Arab writer made his line still rule as far afield as Minnagara near the Indus delta. On the Bactrian side the Alexander-descent used to be claimed by the ruling families, now mostly extinct,[2] in Wakhan, Darwas, Karategin, Roshan, Shignan, Pokhpu, Ferghana, and Badakshan, celebrated by Marco Polo; in Margelan of Ferghana his red silk banner used to be shown, and his tomb honoured as a shrine; the Mirs of Badakshan used to cherish a debased Greek patera, now in London, as an heirloom, and their very horses descended from Bucephalus. In the Indian North-west innumerable stories

1 For a full examination of the Alexander-descents see Tarn, op. cit. pp. 301–3, 408, 448–9. There can be no real doubt that their original basis was Bactrian Greeks who took to the hills to avoid the nomad conquerors and took with them the fictitious Seleucid pedigree beginning with Alexander.
2 If any survive they must be Soviet citizens.

attach to his name; some may be folk-memory, but some are Graeco-Bactrian, Islamite, or even later; at least one new one has appeared under British rule.[1] But all the countries claimed him as theirs. In Persian story he became a son of Ochus by Philip's daughter; in Egyptian, a son of the last native Pharaoh, the magician Nectanebo, who in the guise of Ammon had deceived Olympias. In Jewish legend he was the Two-horned, the precursor of the Messiah; and as Dhulcarnein, the Two-horned, he became one of the heroes of Islam. The Bedouin thought that Napoleon was Iskander come again; in France he ended as a knight of chivalry, in Abyssinia as a Christian saint.

Hardly was he dead when legend became busy with his terrible name, and strove to give him that world-kingdom which he never sought in life. Around him the whole dream-world of the East took shape and substance; of him every old story of a divine world-conqueror was told afresh. More than eighty versions of the Alexander-romance, in twenty-four languages, have been collected, some of them the wildest of fairy-tales; they range from Britain to Malaya; no other story in the world has spread like his. Long before Islam the Byzantines knew that he had traversed the Silk Route and founded Chubdan, the great Han capital of Sian-fu; while the Graeco-Egyptian Romance made him subdue both Rome and Carthage, and compensated him for his failure to reach the eastern Ocean by taking him through the gold and silver pillars of his ancestor Heracles to sail the western. In Jewish lore he becomes master of the Throne of Solomon, and the High Priest announces him as ruler of the fourth world-kingdom

[1] Sir A. Stein, *Archaeological Reconnaissances in N.W. India and S.E. Iran,* 1937, p. 32, n. 15.

of Daniel's prophecy; he shuts up Gog and Magog behind
the Iron Gate of Dariel,[1] and bears on his shoulders the
hopes of the whole earth; one thing alone is forbidden
him, to enter the cloud-girdled Earthly Paradise. The
national legend of Iran, in which the man who in fact
brought the first knowledge of the Avesta to Europe
persecutes the fire-worshippers and burns the sacred book,
withers away before the romance of the world-ruler; in
Persian story he conquers India, crosses Thibet, and sub-
dues the Faghfur of China with all his dependencies; then
he turns and goes northward across Russia till he comes to
the Land of Darkness. But Babylon, as was fitting, took
him farthest; for the Babylon-inspired section of the
Romance knows that he passed beyond the Darkness and
reached the Well of Life at the world's end, on the shores of
the furthest ocean of them all.

The real impress that he left on the world was far
different; for, whatever else he was, he was one of the
supreme fertilising forces of history. He lifted the civilised
world out of one groove and set it in another; he started
a new epoch; nothing could again be as it had been. He
greatly enlarged the bounds of knowledge and of human
endeavour, and gave to Greek science and Greek civilisation a scope and an opportunity such as they had never yet
possessed. Particularism was replaced by the idea of the
'inhabited world', the common possession of civilised men;
trade and commerce were internationalised, and the 'inhabited world' bound together by a network both of new
routes and cities, and of common interests. Greek culture,
heretofore practically confined to Greeks, spread through-

---

1 A. R. Anderson, *Alexander's Gate, Gog and Magog, and the Enclosed Nations*,
1932, p. 59: Dariel, not Derbend.

out that world; and for the use of its inhabitants, in place of the many dialects of Greece, there grew up the form of Greek known as the *koinē*, the 'common speech'. The Greece that taught Rome was the Hellenistic world which Alexander made; the old Greece counted for little till modern scholars re-created Periclean Athens. So far as the modern world derives its civilisation from Greece, it largely owes it to Alexander that it had the opportunity. If he could not fuse races, he transcended the national State; and to transcend national States meant to transcend national cults; men came to feel after the unity which must lie beneath the various religions. Outwardly, this unity was ultimately satisfied in the official worship of the Roman Emperor, which derived from the worship of Alexander after his death; but beside this external form there grew up in men's hearts the longing for a true spiritual unity. And it was Alexander who created the medium in which the idea, when it came, was to spread. For it was due to him that Greek civilisation penetrated western Asia; and even if much of the actual work was done by his successors, he broke the path; without him they would not have been. Consequently, when at last Christianity showed the way to that spiritual unity after which men were feeling, there was ready to hand a medium for the new religion to spread in, the common Hellenistic civilisation of the 'inhabited world'; without that, the conquests made by Christianity might have been as slow and difficult as they became when the bounds of that common civilisation were overpassed.

But if the things he did were great, one thing he dreamt was greater. We may put it that he found the Ideal State of Aristotle, and substituted the Ideal State of Zeno. It was not merely that he overthrew the narrow restraints of the former, and, in place of limiting men by their opportunity, created opportunities adequate for men in a world where none need be a pauper and restrictions on population were meaningless. Aristotle's State had still cared nothing for humanity outside its own borders; the stranger must still be a serf or an enemy. Alexander changed all that. When he declared that all men were alike sons of one Father, and when at Opis he prayed that Macedonians and Persians might be partners in the commonwealth and that the peoples of his world might live in harmony and in unity of heart and mind,[1] he proclaimed for the first time the unity and brotherhood of mankind. Perhaps he gave no thought to the slave world—we do not know; but he, first of all men, was ready to transcend national differences, and to declare, as St Paul was to declare, that there was neither Greek nor barbarian. And the impulse of this mighty revelation was continued by men who did give some thought to the slave world; for Zeno, who treated his slave as himself, and Seneca, who called himself the fellow-slave of his slaves, would (though Alexander might not) have understood St Paul when he added 'there is neither bond nor free'. Before Alexander, men's dreams of the ideal state had still been based on class-rule and slavery; but after him comes Iambulus' great Sun-State, founded on brotherhood and the dignity of free labour. Above all, Alexander inspired Zeno's vision of a world in which all men should be members one of another, citizens of one State without distinction of race or institutions, subject only to and in harmony with the Common Law immanent in the Universe, and united in one social life not by compulsion but

1 See App. 25, VI, and pp. 116–7 ante.

only by their own willing consent, or (as he put it) by Love. The splendour of this hopeless dream may remind us that not one but two of the great lines of social-political thought which until recently divided the world go back to Alexander of Macedon. For if, as many believe, there was a line of descent from his claim to divinity, through Roman Emperor and medieval Pope, to the great despotisms of yesterday, despotisms 'by the grace of God', there is certainly a line of descent from his prayer at Opis, through the Stoics and one portion of the Christian ideal, to that brotherhood of all men which was proclaimed, though only proclaimed, in the French Revolution. The torch Alexander lit for long only smouldered; perhaps it still only smoulders to-day; but it never has been, and never can be, quite put out.[1]

1 I have left the latter part of this paragraph substantially as written in 1926. Since then we have seen new and monstrous births, and are still moving in a world not realised; and I do not know how to rewrite it.

INDEX

Abisares, 92, 97, 100
Abreas, 102
Abydos, 22
Abyssinia, 144
Acesines, 92
Achaemenid(s), 54, 86, 99, 111, 122
Achilles, 2, 15, 100, 124
Acrocorinthus, 128
Ada, 19, 20
Adrianople, 5
Adriatic, 127
Aegean, 32, 42, 79, 128, 139
Aeolian cities, 18, 134
Aeropus, 3
Aeschylus, 85
Aetolia, 4, 6, 7
Agathocles of Bactria, 140
agēma, of the hypaspists, 10, 39, 115; of the Companions, 83–4, 92, 94, 101, 106, 111
Agis, 20, 42, 52
Agrianians, 6, 10, 16, 23, 27, 48–50, 68–9, 82, 88, 94, 101, 106–7
Ake, 130
Albanian, 1
Alcetas, 93, 94
Alcimachus, 18
Alexander (see page headings, and passim): as Great King, 39, 54, 59, 60, 62, 84
  his army, at the Dardanelles, 10–13; at Gaugamela, 47–9; for invasion of India, 82–4 (see Agrianians, allies, archers, Bodyguards, Companion cavalry, hypaspists, lancers, phalanx, Staff)
  his coinage, 130–1, 140
  his dream of brotherhood, 146–8

  his Empire, 138–42
  his financial superintendents, 30–1, 35, 44, 52, 56, 128–9
  his Persian policy, 55, 62, 67, 74, 78, 115
  his Persian satraps, 52, 54–5, 61–2, 66, 79, 109, 126; cf. 137
  his policy of fusion, 79, 111, 134, 137–8
  his prayer at Opis, 116–17
  his relations with the Greek world, 111–14, 127–8, 139–42 (see Greek cities)
Alexander-descent, the, 142
Alexander-Romance, the, 122, 134, 144–5
'Alexander's harbour', 106
'Alexander's ladder', 4
Alexander of Epirus, 117
Alexander of Lyncestis, 3, 17, 20–1, 64
Alexandretta, 133
Alexandria (Egypt), 12, 41, 130, 133–4, 135n.
Alexandria, description of an, 134–6
Alexandria, of the Arians, 61; A. in Arachosia, 65; A. Bactra, 76, 133; A. Bucephala, 97; A. in Carmania, 109; A. of the Caucasus, 65, 88; A. the Farthest, 68; A. by Issus, 130; A. in Makarene, 107; A. Merv, 76; A. Nicaea, 97; A. on the Oxus, 76; A. in Seistan, 64; A. of the Tigris, 118, 136n.
'Alexandrians, the', 135
Alexandrias, 104, 127, 133
Alexandria Troas, 133
Alinda, 19
Amanic Gates, 24, 25

149

Index

Amanis river, 108
Amanus, 24, 26
Ambhi, 88
Ambracia, 4, 5
American(s), 43, 141
Amisus, 35
Ammon, 42-4, 77-8, 101, 105, 115, 122, 124, 14.'
Ammonias, 42
Amol, 60
Amon-Re, 43
Amon ritual, 122
Amphictyonic League, 139
Amphipolis, 3, 5, 130
Amphoterus, 20, 22, 42
Amyntas, Macedonian exile, 24, 26-8
Amyntas, phalanx leader, 11, 48, 52, 63, 83, 93
Amyntas, satrap of Bactria, 75, 83, 110
Anaxarchus, 13, 75, 77-8
Anaxicrates, 119
Anaxippus, 61
Ancyra, 23
Anderab, 66
Andromachus, 48
Ankara, 23
Antalcidas, Peace of, 22
Antigenes, 93-5
Antigonus [I], as satrap, 11, 18, 21, 29, 124; later, 25, 32, 134
Antigonus Doson, 139n.
Antimenes, 128n., 129
Antiochus I, 73, 137
Antony, 126
Aornos: in Bactria, 66; in India, 90-1, 93
Aorsi, 71
Apama, 73, 111
Apis, 41
Apollo, 43, 67, 77
Apollophanes, 107, 126
Arabia, 108, 118-19
Arabian expedition, the, 120-1
Arabis river, 106

Arachosia, 47, 56, 61, 65-6, 104, 110; 'the Arachosians', 60
Aradus, 36
Aral Sea, 70-1
Aramaic, 86
Aratta, 92, 97-8, 101
Arbela, 51
Arcadia, 6
archers, 10, 16, 23, 68-9, 83, 88, 94, 104-7
Argandab river, 65
Argead kings, 78
Aria, 56, 61, 65-7
Ariarathes, 23, 29, 47
Arigaion, 88
Ariobarzanes, 53
Aristobulus, 12, 75, 103, 109
Aristotle: Alexander's tutor, 1, 2, 9, 13, 122; on the Aral and Caspian, 71, 118; on barbarians, 9, 54; on Callisthenes, 81; the 'god among men', 74, 79-80; his Ideal State, 146-7; on India, 85-7; on kingship, 32; on the Nile, 45; on Ocean, 121; on peace, 55; his researches, 131; his school, 82
Armenia, Armenians, 15, 46, 52, 121, 138
Arrian, 69n., 75, 90n.
Arsames, 61, 66-7, 70
Arses, 37
Arsites, 15, 16
Artabazus, 22, 56-7, 59, 66, 75
Artacoana, 61
Artemis, 33
Arybbas, 12, 52
Asander, 18, 19
Asia, i.e. Persian empire q.v. (meaning, 59n., 85, 87), 2, 5, 41, 79, 111, 113, 115, 127, 129, 130, 132, 134, 137-8, 142, 146; colonisation of, 133
Asia (geographical expression), 1, 13, 22, 25, 85, 127, 136

Asia, lord or king of, 37, 59; autocrat of, 79, 113, 138
Asia Minor, 9, 13–15, 17, 36, 56, 121, 134, 138; Alexander's arrangements for, 28–31. *See* Greek cities of Asia Minor
Asoka, 142
Aspasii, 88
Aspendus, 21, 35
Assaceni, 89
Astola, 108
Astrabad, 61
Athena, 15, 35
Athenians, 17–19, 22, 36, 42 and n.
Athens, 4–8, 13, 17, 22, 45, 52, 54, 114, 146; coinage of, 130; policy of, 6, 19, 22, 60, 113–14
Athos, Mt, 41
Atizyes, 15
Atropates, 75, 109, 137
Attalus: Philip's general, 3, 4; Alexander's general, 93–4
Attic standard, 130
Attock, 92
Austanes, 75–6
Autariatae, 6
Autophradates, 59, 75
Avesta, 145
Azemilk, 35
Azov, Sea of, 71

Babylon: Alexander at, 51–2, 54, 117–18; his death at, 120, cf. 110; 127, 130–2, 139, 141, 145
Babylonia, 118; canal system, 119, 132
Bactra, 13, 48, 60, 66–7, 72, 76, 87, 112; Alexander's winter at, 70, 71, 77–80
Bactria, 47, 56, 61, 65–6, 71–2, 75–6, 82–3, 110, 138, 140, 142
Bactrian Greeks, 143n.; horse, 46, 49, 51, 127; satrapy, 127
Bactrians, 56, 61, 66

Badakshan, 142
Bāhlīkas, 90n.
Bahrein, 119
Bajaur: district, 88–9; town, 88
Balacrus: Bodyguard, 12, 28. An officer, 48, 83
Balkan(s), 4, 11, 130; Balkan cavalry, 84
Balkh, 61
Bampur river, 108
Bamyan, 66, 88
Bandar Gäz, 59
Barsaëntes, 47, 56–7, 61
Bar-sar, 91
Barsine, 111
Batis, 41
Bazira, 90
Beas river, 98–100, 126
Bedouin, 144
bematists, 13, 69, cf. 107
Berber blood, 137
Bessus, 47, 49–51, 56–7, 59, 61, 65–7, 70, 87
Bimber, 92
Birkot, 90n.
Bithynia, 29
Black Sea, 71, 127, 139
Bodyguards, 12, 14, 20, 28, 52, 63, 83, 105, 110
Boeotia, 7
Bokhara, 70
Brahmans, 92, 102–4
Branchidae, 67
Britain, 141, 144
British, 138, 142, 144
Bruttians, 117
Bucephalus, 142, cf. 97
Buddhism, 142
Bujnurd, 61
Buldur, Lake, 21
Bulgaria, 5
Buner (district and river), 91
Būrimār ravine, 91
Byblus, 37, 130
Byzantine(s), 5, 144

Index

Cabul river, 88
Cadmea, 6, 8, 140
Cadusians, 46, 121
Calanus, 110
Calas, 11, 17, 23, 26, 28–9
Callisthenes, 13, 42, 63, 86; at
    Bactra, 77–8, 80–1; death, 81–2
Candahar, 65n., 108
Cappadocia, Cappadocians, 15, 23,
    27, 29, 46, 121, 138
Cardaces, 15, 25, 26–7, 45
Caria, 19, 20–1, 26, 87, 139
Carmania, 65, 108–10
Carrhae, 69
Carthage, Carthaginians, 40, 121,
    144
Caspian Gates, 56
Caspian Sea, 59, 60, 71, 121
Cassander, 3, 12, 82, 120, 124, 133
Catanes, 75–6
Cathaeans, 92, 97–8
'Caucasus', 66
Celaenae, 21
Celts, 5, 6, 86
Chaeronea, 2, 52
Chalcedon, 35, 60
Chalcidice, 10
Chalcis, 8, 140
Chaldean, 119
Chandragupta, 100, 103, 105, 142
Charax-Mesene, 118
Chares, 79, 82
Charidemus, 8
Chenab river, 92, 97, 101–3
China, 85, 142, 145
Chinese Turkestan, 85
Chios, Chians, 22, 31, 33–4, 42, 45
Chitral, 142
Chodjend, 68–70
Chorasmii, 70
Chorienes, 72n., 75–6
Christian, Christianity, 144, 146, 148
Chubdan, 144
Cilicia, 23–4, 28–9, 38, 139; mints,
    130–1

Cilician Gates, 23
Cius, 35
Clazomenae, 132
Cleander, 48–9, 64, 84, 109, 130
Cleitarchus, 71
Cleitus the Black, 11, 17, 64, 83;
    murder of, 73–5, 123
Cleitus of Illyria, 6
Cleitus the White, 83, 93–4, 101
Cleomenes, 44, 109, 129, 130n.
Cleopatra, 3, 4
Climax, Mt, 21, 77–8, 81
Cocala, 107–8
Coenus, phalanx-leader, 11, 39, 48,
    72–3, 83; hipparch, 91, 93–4,
    96–7, 109; death, 101
Columbus, 43, 121
Companions, the, 12
Companions, i.e. the Companion
    cavalry, 11, 12, 16–17, 27, 57,
    63, 68–9, 72, 94, 101, 106
    at Gaugamela, 48–9, 50–1
    reorganised, 64, 83–4, 88, 92–3,
    117
Copais, Lake, 132
Corinth, 3, 5, 8, 140; see League of
    Corinth
Cos, 42
Cossaeans, 117
Crassus, 69, 126
Craterus: phalanx-leader, 11, 20, 48,
    50; independent commands, 53,
    59, 61, 63, 72, 76; Alexander's
    second in command, 88; in
    India, 93–7, 101, 108–9; pro-
    posed mission to Europe, 112–
    13, 115–17
Crete, Cretan, 3, 42, 100; Cretan
    archers, 10, 101; see archers
Cydnus river, 23
Cynics, 2, 13
Cyprian kings, 139; mints, 130
Cyprians, 19, 38–40
Cyprus, 67, 87
Cyrene, 42–3, 137

Index

Cyropolis, 40, 67–8
Cyrus, 65, 87, 109, 124
Cyrus the younger, 21
Cyzicus, 14, 35, 139

Dahae, 66
Damascus, 24, 36, 41, 130
Daniel, 145
Danube, 5, 71
Dardanelles, 8, 10, 15, 17, 23, 37, 62–3, 84
Dariel, 145
Darius I, 68, 70, 85–7, 98, 126
Darius III; 6, 8, 15, 20, 22–3, 32, 35, 44, 60, 75, 116; Issus campaign, 23–5, 27–8; correspondence with Alexander, 36–7, 40–1; Gaugamela campaign, 45, 47, 50–1; flight and murder, 56–7, cf. 61, 70; character, 58; his family, 28, 52, 110; his treasure, 53, 130, 132
Darkness, land of, 145
Darwas, 143
Deinocrates, 12, 41
Deli river, 24
Delphi, 5, 14, 34, 42–3, 124
Delta (Indus), 105
Demades, 8, 81n.
Demaratus, 3
Demetrius: of Bactria, 138; Bodyguard, 12, 63; hipparch, 93–4; of Phalerum, 82
Demosthenes, 6
Derbent, 75
Dhulcarnein, 144
Diades, 12
Didyma, 77
Dikaiomata, 135n.
Diodotus, 140
Dionysius of Heraclea, 35
Dionysus, 74, 89, 90, 109, 113n.
Dium, 17
Dodona, 42
Dominions, the, 141

Doura-Europus, 136
Drangiana, 61, 65
Drapsaka, 66
Drypetis, 111
Dyrta, 91

Earthly Paradise, the, 145
Eastern Hindustan, 85
Eastern Iran, 56, 60–1; Eastern Iranian horse, 84, 92. See Iran
Ecbatana, 54, 56, 70, 117
Egypt, 25, 36, 54, 86–7, 109, 118, 129, 138, 140; Alexander in, 41, 43–4; Egyptians, 43
Elburz Mts, 59
Elephantine, 42
elephants, 47, 88, 92–7, 101, 104, 110, 125
Elis, 6
Elymiotis, 3
Embolima, 90
Ephesus, Ephesians, 18, 33
Ephippus, 73
Ephorus, 86
Epirus, 4, 117
Eratosthenes, 55, 116
Eresus, 34
Erigyius, 66
Erythrae, 31, 77, 132
E-Sagila, 54, 132
Ethiopia, 85–6
Etruscans, 117
Eudamus, 104, 110
Eumenes of Cardia, 13, 115, 117, 134
Euphrates river, 21, 25, 40, 45–6, 106, 119
Euripides, 1
Europe, 41, 52, 70, 110, 134, 145
European(s), 25, 72, 83–4, 134, 138
Euthydemus, 140

Faisabad, 76
Faranj, 62
Ferghana, 142
France, 144

Index

Fravartish, 70
French Revolution, 148
Further India, 85

Gandaridae, 98–9
Gandhāra, 85–7, 90, 94, 104
Ganges river, 85, 99
Gaugamela, 11, 37, 44, 52, 112; battle of, 46–51; see 56–7
Gaza, 40–1, 130
Gedrosia, 65, 84n., 104, 106, 110, 126
Getae, 5
Ghorband river, 65–6, 87
Gilan, 121
Gilgit, 142
Glaucias, 6
Gog, 145
Gordias, 21
Gordium, 21, 23
Gorgias, 93–4
Graeco-Bactrian(s), 127, 144
Graeco-Egyptian, 144
Graeco-Macedonian, 141
Granicus, battle of, 16–17, cf. 26, 31, 74
Greece, 4–6, 10, 19, 22, 25, 37, 42, 56, 109, 112, 120, 127, 129, 138
Greek allies (League troops), 10, 11, 16–17, 19, 20, 26–7, 48, 54, 131
Greek cities of Asia Minor, 13–14, 17, 31–6, 54, 79, 112, 127, 136; see Asia Minor
(new), 134–6, 141; see Alexandria of the League of Corinth, 112–14, 127–8, 139–41; see League of Corinth
Greek, civilisation, 134, 145–6; corporations, 135; culture, 134, 138, 140, 145; democracies, 17–18, 112; dialects, 146; freedom, 32, 113, cf. 139–40; hoplites, 26, 46, 125; law and law-courts, 135–6; officials, 135; science, 145; seers, 116

Greek mercenaries (Alexander's), 10, 21, 26, 27, 68, 70, 83, 106–7, 110, 134; at Gaugamela, 48–51
Greek mercenaries (Darius'), 15–17, 22–3, 44–5; at Issus, 25–8 (see 52–3, 83); at Gaugamela, 47, 50–1; later, 56–7, 59–60
Greeks, 8, 10, 17, 48, 52, 54, 60, 70, 74, 79, 81, 99, 101, 114, 116, 127–8, 134, 136–8, 140
Greeks and barbarians, 9, 54–5, 147
Gulashkird, 108–9
Gurdaspur, 98
Gurgan river, 61
Gwadur, 108

Hab river, 106
Hadramaut, 119
Haemus, 5
Hakra channel, 104
Halicarnassus, 16, 18–20
Halil Rud river, 108
Han dynasty, 142, 144
Hannibal, 125
Hapsburgs, 141
Harpalus, 3, 11–12, 56, 62, 93, 109, 128–9, 132, 141
Hazāra, 100
Hegelochus, 22, 42
Hellas, 8, 36
Hellenes, 113
Hellenic alliance, 60; 'life and training', 136
Hellenistic world, 146
Hellespontine Phrygia, 15, 17
Helmund river, 65
Hephaestion, 12, 52; hipparch, 64, 72, 80, 83; commands in India, 88, 90, 92–4, 97, 101–2; marriage, 111; death and honours, 117, 131–2
Heracleia (in Bithynia), 35, 121
Heracleides, 118

154

Index

Heracles, 2, 37, 43, 78, 90, 101, 124, 129, 144
Herat, 61
Hermolaus, 81
Herodotus, 71 n., 85, 87 n., 137
Hieron of Soli, 119
High Priests, 139, 144
Hindu Kush, 66, 86–7, 138, 142
Hingol river, 107
Homonoia, 117, 122
Hunza, 142
Hydaspes, battle of the, 93–6
Hydaspes river, 92–3
Hydraotes river, 97
Hypaspists, 10, 16, 23, 27, 48–9, 82, 87–8, 91, 95, 101, 106, 115
Hypereides, 114
Hyphasis river, 98
Hyrcania, 59, 137
Hyrcanian Sea, 71, 118

Iambulus, 147
Idrieus, 19
Iliad, 2
Ilian League, 32
Ilium, 15, 103, 132
Illyria, 3, 6; Illyrian(s), 1, 25, 120
India, 25, 71, 110, 117–19, 126, 130, 142, 145; meaning of, 85–7; invasion of, 82–4, 97, 99, 125
India, northern, 103, 138; the North-West, 143
Indian belt west of Indus, 104–5, cf. 127
Indian, contingents, 94; customs, 107; hill-tribes, 125; history, 142; mercenaries, 89; peninsula, 85; princes, 84, 101, 131–2; rivers, 105; satrapies (Alexander's), 104–5, 110
Indian Ocean, 85–6, 105
Indians, 46, 50, 61, 86, 90–1, 104, 142
Indus river, 85–6, 88–93, 97, 101, 103–6; delta, 143

Ionia, 17
Ionian League, 32
Iran, 15, 56, 85, 104, 127, 140, 145 (*see* Eastern Iran)
Iranian(s), 53, 55, 60, 84, 90 n., 106, 111, 116, 134, 137, 139, 141
Isaurians, 29
Iskander, 144
Isker river, 5
Islam, Islamite, 144
Isocrates, 8, 9, 36, 79, 132
Issus, 24, 34, 36, 56–7, 83, 126; battle of, 24–7, 40
Italy, 117, 139

Jalalpur, 93 n.
Jaxartes, 46, 67–8, 85, 121
Jerusalem, 41 and n.
Jewish legend, 144
Jhelum river, 84, 92, 97–8, 100–1, 125; town, 93–4
Jonah pass, 26 (*see* Pillar of Jonah)
Journal, the, 13, 25, 119, 120 and n.

Kafiristan, Kafirs, 142
Kajan pass, 5
Kalat, 105
Kamdesh Kafirs, 89
Kaoshan pass, 87
Kara-kapu pass, 24
Karategin, 142
Kashaf-Rud river, 61
Kashmir, 92
Kathiawar, 138
Keramlais, 46
Khajir river, 46
Kharoshthī, 86
Khawak pass, 66
Khyber pass, 88
King's land, 14, 30, 34, 135–6
Kirghiz, 69
Koh-i-Mor, 89
koinē, the, 146
Koja-Balkan pass, 5
Krishna, 90

155

Ksudraka, 102
Kunar river, 88, 90, 104–5
Kurachi, 106, 108
Kwarizm, 70

Laghman, 88
Lagos (*see* Ptolemy)
Lampsacus, 15
lancers, 11, 16–17, 27, 48–9, 50, 57
Lanice, 74
Laomedon, 12
Las Bela, 106
League of Corinth, the, 4–5, 10, 19,
    31, 34, 37, 52–4, 60, 127, 139;
    fleet of, 14, 18, 34
Leonnatus, 28, 52, 88, 102–3, 107–8
Lesbos, 22, 42
Libyan(s), 117, 137
Lindus, 59
lion-gryphon, 59
London, 142
Longarus, 6
Lucanians, 117
Luristan, 117
Lut, the, 108
Lycaonia, 29
Lycia, Lycian, 20–1, 35, 38, 68
Lydia, Lydians, 15, 18, 139
Lyncestis, Lyncestian, *see* Alexander
    of Lyncestis
Lysimachus, 12, 110, 124
Lysippus, 2

Macedonia, 1, 4–6, 10, 14, 17, 20, 25,
    36–7, 48, 52, 59, 88, 115, 127,
    138–9
Macedonian, customs, 63, 81, 116;
    exiles, 20, 24; garrisons (in
    Greek cities), 4, 8, 33–5, 128,
    140; training, 77, 111; troops,
    10, 22, 40, 48, 52, 63, 74, 91, 96,
    102, 115–16, 131, 142 (*see* Com-
    panion cavalry, hypaspists, pha-
    lanx)
Macedonian State, 139, cf. 138

Macedonians, 55, 73, 79, 80, 101,
    110–11, 115–16, 124, 134–5,
    137–8, 147
Maeotis, 71
Magadha, 99
Magi, 116
Magog, 145
Mahlava, 101
Makran, 106
Malaya, 144
Malli, 92, 101–4
Mallus, 35
Maracanda, 60, 67–70, 72–3
Marathus, 8, 36–7
Mardi, 61
Margelan, 142
Massaga, 89, 125
Massagetae, 69, 72–3
Mausolus, 19
Mazaeus, 45–7, 50–2, 54, 56
Medes, 46
Media, 54–5, 75, 109, 127
Media Paraetacene, 55, 109, 127
Mediterranean, 42, 122, 131
Megalopolis (battle of), 28, 52
Megasthenes, 85
Meleager, 11, 83, 93–4
Melkart, 37, 40
Memnon, 8, 15–17; his command,
    18–20, 33, 42; death, 22
Memoirs (Alexander's supposed),
    122
Memphis, 41, 43–4
Menes, 28, 52
Menidas, 48–9, 64
Menon, 65
Mentor, 23
Meros, Mt, 89
Merv, 76
Meshed, 61
Mesopotamians, 46
Messiah, the, 144
Methymna, 22
Mieza, 2
Miletus, 16, 18, 32, 137

Index

Milyad, 20-1
Minnagara, 142
Mithridates (of Cius), 35
Mithrines, 18, 52
Mithrobarzanes, 15
Mitylene, 19, 22, 31-2
Mulla pass, 104
Multān, 102
Murghab river, 61
Myriandrus, 24
Mysians, 28

Nabarzanes, 26, 56-7, 59, 61
Nad Ali, 62
Nagir, 142
Napoleon, 125, 144
Naucratis, 44
Nautaka, 72, 75
Nazretabad, 108
Nearchus, 3, 12; satrap, 21, 83, 85;
    as admiral, 87, 99, 100, 105,
    120; voyage, 108, 118-19
Nebuchadrezzar, 37, 120
Nectanebo, 144
Nelson, 51
Nicanor, Parmenion's son, 11, 62
Nicanor, a satrap, 87, 90, 104
Nile, 86
Nisaea, 109
nomads, 68-9
Nysa, Nysaeans, 89-90

Ocean, 85, 87, 99, 100-1, 118-21,
    144-5
Ochus (Artaxerxes III), 19, 37, 86, 144
Odrysians, 48
Ohind, 92
Olbia, 71
Old Tyre, 37
Olympians, 100
Olympias, 1-4, 10, 62, 112, 117, 123,
    144
Olympic games, 111
Olynthus, 13, 73, 77
Onesicritus, 13, 85, 101

Opiane, 65
Opis, 115, 147-8
Ora: in Swat, 90; in Makarene, 107
Orchomenus, 7, 8
Oreitae, 106-7, 110, 127
Ormuz, straits of, 108
Orontopates, 20
Ossa, 4
Oxus river, 66-8, 70-1, 76
Oxyartes, 66, 72n., 75-6, 88, 137
Oxydracae, 92, 102-4

Paeonians, 11, 16, 48-9, 57
Pages' conspiracy, 81
Palestine, 41
Pallakopas cut, 119
Pamphylia, 20-1, 77
Panhellenic ideas, 8, 81; policy, 18
Panjkora river, 89
Panjshir river, 66
Paphlagonia, 23, 29, 121
Paraetacene: (in Sogdiana), 75; the
    Median, 55, 109, 127
Paraetonium, 43
Parmenion, Philip's general, 3, 8;
    Alexander's second in com-
    mand, 11, 15, 20-1, 24, 36, 41,
    45-6, 53; at Gaugamela, 48,
    50-1, 63; his advice rejected,
    16, 18, 23-4, 40, 54, 63; on
    communications, 55, 62; his
    murder, 64, 125. See 74, 83-4,
    124
'Parnassus', 85
Paropamisadae, 65, 85-6, 88, 104-5,
    137n.
Paropamisus, 46, 66, 85
Parthava, see Parthians
Parthia, 59, 127, 137
Parthians (Parthava), 46, 50-1;
    'Parthian' tactics, 69
Pasargadae, 53
Pasni, 108
Patala, 104-5, 132
Pātaliputra, 138

Paurava, 92
Pedieis, 14
Peithon: satrap, 105; the Body-guard, 124
Pelion (in Illyria), 6, 7
Pella, 130
Peloponnese, 4
Perdiccas, 7, 11, 29; Bodyguard, 83, 88; hipparch, 93–4, 98, 102–3; acting vizier, 121, 124
Perge, 21
Perinthus, 37
Peripatetic literature, 80; school, 82
Persepolis, 53–4, 58, 60
Perseus, 43
Persia, 37, 54, 87, 98, 119, 126, 141; invasion of, 8, 9
Persian army, 14; at Issus, 25; at Gaugamela, 46–51; Persian archers, 14, 26–7, 45–6; cavalry, 15, 26, 45, 47, 49–51, 125, *see* Bactrian, Iranian; chiliarch, 26, 57, 117; command, 24, 45; Guard, the (cavalry), 46, 50–1; Guard, the (infantry), 27, 47, 50; leaders, 16, 115; light-armed, 26–7, 120
Persian army (Alexander's), 115
Persian, captives, 123, cf. 28; cere-monial, 79–81; coin-standard, 35; dress, 79, 110–11; envoys, 1; language, 12, 99, 110; nobles, 17, 27, 54, 83, 111; numbers, 25, cf. 125; officials, 86; roads, 126; sphere, 102; story, 144–5
Persian, empire, 9, 15, 25, 36, 54, 87, 110, 121; coinage, 130; financial basis, 30; land system, 15, 30, 60; rule, 17, 29, 67; tribute, 15, 18, 31
Persian fleet, 18, 21–3, 32, 36–8, 45
Persian Gates, the, 53
Persian Gulf, the, 99, 105–6, 118–19
Persians, 15, 23, 29, 37, 55, 79, 81, 101, 110, 116, 135, 141, 147

'Persians, the', 60
Persis, 53–4, 109–10, 127
Peucela, Peucelaïtis, 90n.
Peucestas, 102, 110–11
Peuke, 5
phalangites, 57, 69
phalanx, 10, 16, 27–8, 48, 50, 88–9, 91, 93–5, 98, 104, 106; enlarged, 82–3
Pharaoh(s), 41, 43–4, 78, 122, 140, 144
Pharasmanes, 70–1
Pharnabazus, 22–3, 38, 42, 46
Pharnuches, 68–9
Phaselis, 20–1, 35
Philip II, 1–6, 8, 11, 37, 55, 59, 62, 74, 78–9, 125, 127, 132, 140, 144; coinage, 130
Philip III, 140
Philippus of Acarnania, 23–4
Philippus, Harpalus' brother, 93, 97, 101, 104
Philippus, satrap of Bactria, 110
Philotas, 11, 74; treason and execu-tion of, 62–4
Philoxenus, 31, 56
Phocion, 8
Phocis, Phocians, 7
Phoenicia, Phoenicians, 19, 23, 36, 38–40, 52, 87, 119, 130–1, 138; Phoenician standard, 130
Phrada, 62–5
Phrataphernes, 59, 70, 75, 139
Phrygia, Phrygians, 14–15, 20–1, 26
'Pillar of Jonah' pass, 24
Pinarus river, 24
Pindar, 7, 42
Pīr-sar, 91
Pisidia, 20–1, 29
Pixodarus, 19, 20
Plataea, 7, 8
Plato on barbarians, 9
Plutarch, 80, 82, 84, 123
Pnytagoras, 38–9
Pokhpu, 143

Polydamas, 64
Polyperchon, 28, 50, 83, 93–4
Polytimetus river, 69, 70
Pontus, 121
Portipora, 60
Porus, 87, 92–8, 100, 122, 125
Poseidon, 101, 105
Priene, 14, 18, 34–5
Prophthasia, 64
proskynesis, 77, 79–80; *see* prostration
prostration, 79–80, 113
Psois, 43 n.
Ptolemaeus: Bodyguard, 12, 14, 20;
    an officer, 20
Ptolemais, 134
Ptolemy [I], son of Lagos, 3, 12, 44,
    64, 67, 74, 88, 91, 102, 124, 134;
    as historian, 13, 25, 43 n., 47 n.,
    63, 81, 90 n., 94, 120 n.
Ptolemy (geographer), 87 n.
Punjab, 85, 87, 92, 98–9, 103, 121–2,
    126
Pura, 108
Purali river, 104–5
Pushkalāvatī, 90
Pyrrhon, 13
Pythia, the, 5

Quetta, 105

Rajauri, 92
Rajputana, 85
Ran of Cutch, 104–5
Ras Mussendam, 108, 119
Ravi river, 97, 101–2
Rei, 56
Reis tribes, 65
Rhacotis, 41
Rhagae, 56
Rhodes, 31, 34, 38
Rhodope, 5
Roman Emperor, 146, 148; im-
    perialism, 141
Rome, 121, 124, 126
Roshan, 142

Roxane, 76, 134
Royal pages, 13
Royal road, 29
Russia, 145

Sabiktas, 23
Saca, Sacas, 46–7, 49, 68–9, 125
Sagala, 98
Sagalassus, 21
St Paul, 147
Salaminia, 42
Salamis.(in Cyprus), 38
Salmacis, 20
Salonica, 133
Samārah lake, 105
Samarcand, 67, 77, 133
Samos, Samians, 31, 113
Sandar Bār, 102
Sangala, 98
Sarapis, 43 n., 120 n.
Sardis, 18, 36, 52, 132
Sasigupta, 87, 91
Satibarzanes, 56–7, 61, 66
Sceptic school, 13
Scylax, 86
scythed chariots, 46–9
Scythians, 68, 71
Seistan lake, 108
Seleucid kings, 73, 127, 133, 138;
    eparchies, 127
Seleucid pedigree, the fictitious,
    140 n., 143 n.
Seleucus, 12, 73, 83, 105, 120, 138;
    in the Hydaspes battle, 95–6;
    his marriage, 111
Selge, 35
Semiramis, 124
Seneca, 147
Serbia, 6
Shāhkōt pass, 90
Shahrud, 56, 59
Shignan, 142
Shipka pass, 5
Sialcot, 98
Sian-fu, 133, 144

Siberia, 85
Sibyrtius, 110
Side, 21, 35
Sidon, 37-8, 40, 118, 130
Sidonians, 39
Silistria, 5
Silk Route, 144
Simmias, 48, 50
Sind, 85-6, 97, 104-5
Sinope, 35
Sistovo, 5
Sisygambis, 28
Sitalces, 64, 109
Șiva, 89
Siwah, 42
Smyrna, 133
Sochi, 24
Sogdiana, 47, 66-7, 70-2, 75, 137
Sogdian(s), 67, 69, 72-3, 138;
    'Sogdian rock', the, 75
Soli: in Cilicia, 35; in Cyprus, 67;
    doubtful, 119
Solomon, 144
Sparta, Spartans: not in the League,
    5, 7, 17, 19-20; hostile to Mace-
    donia, 28, 36-7, 42, 45; defeated
    by Antipater, 52-3, 60, 83;
    deify Alexander, 113
Spitamenes, 66-70, 72, 74, 83, 111;
    death, 73
Spithridates, 15, 17
Staff (Alexander's), 11, 12, 28, 52,
    64, 124-5
Stasanor, 12
Stoics, 148
Strymon river, 6
Suez, 119
Susa, 52-3, 71 n., 109-10, 129, 131
Susiana, 109-10
Susians, 46
Sutlej river, 98-9
Swat: district, 89-91, 104; river,
    89
Syria, 15, 24, 41, 45, 119
Syrian Gates, the, 24

Syrians, 46

Taloi range, 107
Tapuria, 59, 60, 75
Tarmita, 76
Tarnak river, 65
Tarsus, 23, 121
Tashkurgan, 66
Taulantini, 6
Taurus Mts, 24, 29, 31
Taxila, 84, 86-8, 92-3, 99
Taxiles, 88, 92, 97, 110
Teheran, 56
Tel Gōmel, 46
Tempe, 4
Temple, the, 41
Tenedos, 22, 31, 42
Termessus, 21
Termez, 76
Thais, 54
Thapsacus, 45-6, 119
Thebans, 7, 36, 111
Thebes, 2, 4, 5, 6, 40, 52; destruction
    of, 7, 8, 125
Themistocles, 137
Theophrastus, 41 n., 82
Thermouthis, 43 n.
Thessalian horse, 4, 11, 16, 20, 36,
    54, 131; at Gaugamela, 48, 50-1
Thessaly, 4, 139
Thibet, 145
Thrace, Thracians, 1, 2, 10, 14, 71,
    120, 135
Thracian troops, 10, 11, 16, 48-9,
    50, 55, 83-4, 104
Throne of Solomon, 144
Thymondas, 23
Tigris river, 46, 118, 133
Timaeus, 82
Tlepolemus, 110
Tomeros river, 107
Triballi, 5
Tripolis, 23, 27
Turkestan, 73, 125
Two-horned, the, 144

Index

Tyre, Tyrians, 12, 19, 37, 41–2, 45, 89, 93, 125; siege of, 38–40; mint, 130

Udegram, 90
Ūṇa-sar, 91
United States, 141
Upper Nile, 44
Uxii, 28 n., 53

Vaksh river, 76
Vedic times, 142

Wakhan, 142
Well of Life, 145
World-conquest, 86, 121, cf. 122, 144

Xenocrates, 2
Xenophon, 43, 87
Xerxes, 36, 51, 54, 132

Yemen, 119
Yusufzai, 90

Zadracarta, 59–60
'Zarangians, the', 62
Zariaspa-Bactra, 66 (see Bactra)
Zelea, 14, 31
Zeno, 146–7; Ideal State of, 147
Zeus, 77–8
Zopyrion, 71
Zoroastrian customs, 86
Zoroastrianism, 140

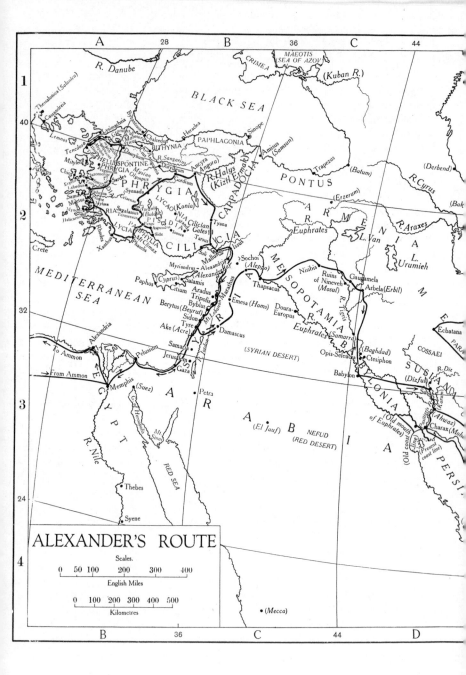

ALEXANDER'S ROUTE

Scales.

0 50 100   200   300   400
English Miles

0 100 200 300 400 500
Kilometres

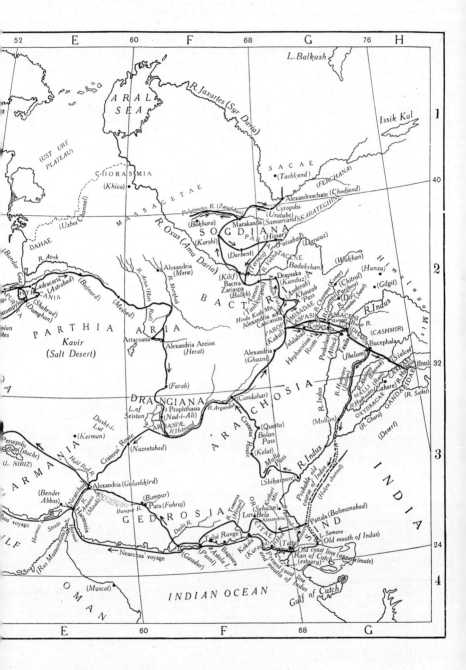

INDEX TO MAP

Abydos, A 1
Acre, B 2
Ahwaz, D 3
Ake, B 2
Akesines, *R.*, GH 2, 3
Aleppo, C 2
Alexandreschate (Chodjend), G 1
Alexandretta, C 2
Alexandria, B 3
Alexandria, C 2
Alexandria, E 3
Alexandria, F 3
Alexandria, G 2
Alexandria ad Caucasum, G 2
Alexandria Areion (Herat), F 2
Alexandria (Merv), F 2
Amanis, *R.*, E 3
Amisus, C 1
Ammon, Road from, AB 3
Ammon, Road to, AB 3
Amol, E 2
Ancyra, B 2
Anderab, G 2
Angora, B 2
Antigoneia, B 1
Aornos, F 2
Arabia, BCD 3
Arachosia, FG 2, 3
Aradus, B 2
Aral Sea, EF 1
Araxes, *R.*, CD 1, 2
Arbela, D 2
Argandab, *R.*, F 3
Aria, F 2
Ariaspae, F 3
Arius, *R.*, F 2
Armenia, CD 2
Artacoana, F 2
Ascania, *L.*, B 2
Aspasii, G 2
Aspendus, B 2
Assaceni, G 2
Astola I., F 3
Astrabad, E 2
Atrek, *R.*, E 2
Attock, G 2
Azov, Sea of, BC 1

Babylon, D 2
Babylonia, CD 2, 3
Bactra-Zariaspa, F 2
Bactria, FG 2
Badakshan, G 2
Baghdad, D 2
Bagisara, F 3
Bahmanabad, G 3
Bahrein I., D 3
Baku, D 1
Balkash, *L.*, G 1
Balkh, F 2
Bampur, F 3
Bampur, *R.*, F 3
Bandar Gaz, E 2
Batum, C 1
Beas, *R.*, H 2
Bender Abbas, E 3
Berytus, B 2
Bithynia, B 1

Black Sea, BC 1
Bokhara, F 2
Bolan Pass, F 3
Bucephala, G 2
Bujnurd, E 2
Buldur, B 2
Burer, *R.*, G 2
Byblus, B 2
Byzantium, B 1

Candahar, F 3
Cappadocia, BC 1, 2
Caria, AB 2
Carmania, E 3
Cashmir, G 2
Caspian Gates, E 2
Caspian Sea, DE 1, 2
Cassandreia, A 1
Cathaei, G 2, 3
Celaenae, B 2
Chalcedon, B 1
Charax, D 3
Chenab, *R.*, G 2
Chios, A 2
Chitral, G 2
Choaspes, *R.* (Kunar), G 2
Chodjend, G 1
Chorasmia, EF 1
Cilicia, BC 2
Cilician Gates, B 2
Citium, B 2
Cius, B 1
Clazomenae, A 2
Climax, *Mt*, B 2
Coast-line, new (Persian Gulf), D 3
Coast-line, old (Persian Gulf), D 3
Coast-line, old (mouth of Indus), G 3
Coast-line, present (mouth of Indus), FG 3, 4
Cophen, *R.*, G 2
Cossaei, D 2
Craterus' Route, EF 3
Crete, A 2
Crimea, B 1
Ctesiphon, D 2
Cutch, Gulf of, G 4
Cutch, Ran of (estuary), G 3
Cyprus, B 2
Cyropolis, G 2
Cyrus, *R.*, CD 1, 2
Cyzicus, B 1

Dahae, E 2
Damascus, C 2
Damghan, E 2
Danube, *R.*, A 1
Darwaz, G 2
Dascylium, B 1
Dasht, *R.*, F 3
Dasht-i-Lut, E 3
Derbend, D 1
Derbent, F 2
Desert, G 3
Diz, *R.*, D 2
Dizful, D 2
Dorylaeum, B 2

Doura-Europus, C 2
Drangiana, F 3
Drapsaka, G 2

Ecbatana, D 2
Egypt, B 3
Elburz Range, DE 2
Emesa, C 2
Ephesus, A 2
Erbil, D 2
Erythrae, A 2
Erzerum, C 2
Euphrates, *R.*, CD 2, 3
Euphrates, Old Mouth of the D 3

Fahraj, F 3
Faisabad, G 2
Farah, F 2
Ferghana, G 1

Gabiene, DE 2
Gandaridae, G 3
Gandhara, G 2
Gaugamela, C 2
Gaza, B 3
Gedrosia, EF 3
Ghara, *R.*, GH 3
Ghazni, G 2
Gilgit, G 2
Gordium, B 2
Gouraios, *R.*, G 2
Granicus, *R.*, A 1
Gulashkird, E 3
Gwadur, F 3

Hab, *R.*, F 3
Hakra Channel, G 3
Halicarnassus, A 2
Halil Rud, *R.*, E 3
Halys, *R.*, BC 1, 2
Hamadan, D 2
Harmozia, E 3
Hecatompylos, E 2
Hellespontine Phrygia, AB 2
Helmund, *R.*, F 3
Hephaestion's Route, G 2
Heraclea, B 1
Herat, F 2
Heri Rud, *R.*, F 2
Heroopolis, G. of, B 3
Himalaya Mts., GH 2
Hindu Kush Mts, FG 2
Hingol, *R.*, F 3
Hissar, G 2
Hormuz I., E 3
Hormuz, Straits of, E 3
Horus, C 2
Hunza, G 2
Hydaspes, *R.*, G 2, 3
Hyderabad, G 3
Hydraotes, *R.*, G 3
Hyphasis, *R.*, GH 3
Hyrcania, E 2

Ilium, A 2
India, G 3
Indian Ocean, F 4
Indus, old mouth of, G 3

Indus, probable old course of, G 3
Indus, *R.*, G 2, 3
Isaura, B 2
Ispahan, D 2
Issik Kul, H 1
Issus, C 2
Istachr, E 3

Jalalabad, G 2
El Jauf, C 3
Jaxartes, *R.* (Syr Daria), FG 1
Jerusalem, B 3
Jhelum, *R.*, G 2, 3
Jordan, *R.*, B 2, 3

Kabul, G 2
Kaoshan Pass, G 2
Karateghin, G 2
Karshi, F 2
Karum, D 2, 3
Kavir (Salt Desert), E 2
Kelat, F 3
Kerman, E 3
Khawak Pass, G 2
Khiva, F 1
Kilif, F 2
Kirthari Mts, F 3
Kizil Ermak, *R.*, BC 1, 2
Kokala, F 3
Konia, B 2
Kuban, *R.*, C 1
Kunduz, G 2
Kurachi, F 3

Lahore, G 3
Lampsacus, A 1
Laranda, B 2
Lebanon, *Mt*, BC 2
Lebedus, A 2
Lemnos, A 2
Lus-Bela, F 3
Lycaonia, B 2
Lycia, B 2
Lydia, AB 2
Lysimacheia, A 1

Maeotis, BC 1
Malli, G 3
Mallus, B 2
Marakanda (Samarcand), F 2
Marathus, C 2
Mardi, D 2
Marmora, Sea of, AB 1
Massaga, G 2
Massagetae, EF 1, 2
Mecca, C 4
Media, DE 2
Mediterranean Sea, AB 2
Memphis, B 3
Merv, F 2
Meshed, E 2
Mesopotamia, C 2
Miletus, A 2
Minab, *R.*, E 3
Mitylene, A 2
Mohammerah, D 3
Mosul, C 2
Mulla Pass, F 3

Multan, G 3
Murghab, *R.*, F 2
Muscat, E 4
Mylasa, A 2
Myndus, A 2
Myriandrus, B 2
Mysian Olympus, B 2

Nad-i-Ali, F 3
Nazretabad, EF 3
Nearchus' voyage, DEF 3
Nefud, C 3
Nile, *R.*, B 3
Nineveh, Ruins of, C 2
Niriz, *L.*, E 3
Nisibis, C 2

Ohind, G 2
Oman, E 4
Opis-Seleucia, D 2
Oreitae, F 3
Oxus, *R.* (Amu Daria), FG 1, 2

Pamphylia, B 2
Panjkora, *R.*, G 2
Paphlagonia, B 1
Paphos, B 2
Paraetacene, D 2
Paraetacene, FG 2
Parium, A 1
Paropamisadae, G 2
Parthia, E 2
Pasargadae, E 3
Pasitigris, *R.*, D 2, 3
Pasni, F 3
Pattala, G 3
Pelusium, B 3
Pergamum, A 2
Perge, B 2
Persepolis, E 3
Persian Gulf, DE 3
Persis, DE 3
Petra, B 3
Peukelaotis, G 2
Phaselis, B 2
Phrygia, B 2
Pisidia, B 2
Polytimetus, *R.* (Zarafshan), FG 2
Pontus, C 1
Priene, A 2
Prophthasia, F 3
Pura, F 3

Quetta, F 3

Ras Mussendam, E 3
Ravi, G 3
Red Desert, C 3
Red Sea, BC 3
Rhagae, D 2
Rhodes, B 2

Sacae, G 1
Sagalassus, B 2
Salamis, B 2
Salonica, A 1
Samara, *L.*, G 3
Samarcand, F 2

Samaria, B 2
Samarra, C 2
Samos, A 2
Samsun, C 1
Sangarius, *R.*, B 1
Sardes, B 2
Sehwan, F 3
Seistan, *L.* of, F 3
Shahrud, E 2
Shikarpore, G 3
Sialcot, G 2
Side, B 2
Sidon, B 2
Sinai, *Mt*, B 3
Sinope, B 1
Smyrna, A 2
Sochoi?, C 2
Sogdiana, FG 2
Soli, B 2
Suastos, *R.*, G 2
Suez, B 3
Susa, D 2
Susiana, D 2, 3
Sutlej, *R.*, GH 3
Swat, *R.*, G 2
Syene, B 3
Synnada, B 2
Syria, BC 2, 3
Syrian Desert, C 2

Taloi Range, F 3
Tapuria, E 2
Tarsus, B 2
Tashkend, G 1
Tashkurgan, F 2
Tatta, F 3
Taxila, G 2
Tenedos, A 2
Teos, A 2
Termessus, B 2
Termez, F 2
Thapsacus, C 2
Thebes, B 3
Thessalonica, A 1
Tomeros, *R.*, F 3
Trapezus, C 1
Tripolis, B 2
Troas, A 2
Tyana, B 2
Tylos, D 3
Tyre, B 2

Uratube, G 2
Urumieh, *L.*, D 2
Ust Urt Plateau, E 1
Uxii, D 3
Uzboi Channel, E 1, 2

·Vakhsh, *R.*, FG 2
Van, *L.*, C 2

Wakhan, G 2

Xanthus, B 2

Zadracarta, E 2
Zarafshan, *R.*, FG 2
Zelea, A 1